More praise for **Invasion from the East**

"This book has much to commend it. Wilson help-
fully draws many distinctions between assumptions
of Eastern-derived religious movements and those of
Christians, and rightly turns Christians back to their
own resources. He also provides helpful background
information on the Hindu, Buddhist, and Taoist traditions. A work for this time, with practical value
for church members."

> Paul V. Martinson
> Luther-Northwestern Seminaries, St. Paul

"Informative, descriptive, sensitive, balanced—a
challenge to our Western minds and faith. Wilson
points to ways we can be enriched in *our* faith,
rather than standing in fear of the invasion from
the East."

> John Schramm
> Holden Village

D1113449

INVASION from the EAST

HOWARD A. WILSON

AUGSBURG Publishing House • Minneapolis

Gu Eilidh
Marti
Martha

Tri ginealaich

Companaich nam
bliadhnachan seo

Contents

Preface

That we are in the midst of a resurgence of religion is clear. What is disturbing to many Christians is that it is not a resurgence of "mainline" Christianity. It is, in fact, taking place on the peripheries of Western religious life. What are Christians to make of the interest in Oriental religious ideas and practices, in mysticism, in the esoteric and the occult? How is it possible that such ideas and practices are finding converts here in the heartland of evangelical Christianity? What spiritual needs are Christians failing to meet that are being met by these practices?

We fear most what we do not understand. To facilitate understanding, this book analyzes the resurgence of religion, identifies its major features, traces their roots in Oriental religious traditions, calls attention to concerns Christians will have with some of these features, and suggests how Christians can learn from those features which attract Westerners today.

Christians have very little to fear from the resurgence of religion, so long as they address it in the biblical prophetic spirit. In fact, this moment in history holds much promise if mainline Christians can find ways to join the resurgence of religion and perhaps recover dimensions in their own tradition that have lain dormant and neglected for centuries.

My friends and colleagues, Dean James A. Bergquist of the Lutheran Theological Seminary and Professor William H. Narum of St. Olaf College, have read the manuscript in various stages of completion and their suggestions have been invaluable. They have given far more than I had any right to ask. Invaluable also was the friendship and unfailing loyalty of my secretary, Mrs. Bernadine Norris.

Chapter 1

Why are Eastern religions making such an impact on Western life?

Over the past several decades the West has been experiencing an invasion from the East. Practices associated with eastern religions have been appearing everywhere.

A young college student named Craig sits cross-legged on the floor of a nondescript building two blocks from the heart of the Michigan State University campus. He is facing a young woman hardly older than himself. It is a long-awaited moment, the beginning of seven steps to bliss, for which he has carefully prepared.

Craig has not eaten since morning. He is about to be given his own mantra by a Transcendental Meditation initiator named Sue. The mantra is a Sanskrit phrase that is to be intoned inwardly to induce meditation. It is to be kept secret, never to be spoken aloud, and it is to be in harmony with the vibrations of the student's personality.

Craig has brought the prescribed offerings. He promises that he has not used drugs for 15 days, and he offers 12 fresh flowers, some fresh fruit, a clean white handkerchief, and a student contribution of $75.

Sue gives Craig his personal mantra and instructs

him in how to use it properly. There follows a little
ceremony in which his offerings are used.

After initiation, Craig begins meditating 15 or 20
minutes in the morning and evening every day. He
has been instructed to sit comfortably and to repeat
the mantra to himself throughout that time. Whenever he is aware of his mind wandering, he is to
bring his attention back to the repetition. The whole
process is to be as effortless as possible.

The result is intended to be more refreshing than
sleep, equipping Craig to use his mental gifts more
effectively and to become more creative. For the first
three days he meets with a small group to discuss his
progress. He is "checked" 10 days later, and may return for help once a month for as long as he feels
the need.

Like all TM practitioners, Craig believes he will
be happier because he has been shown the way to the
basis of his being and to serenity.

Steve and Mary McKensie have sold their home in
the suburbs of New Jersey and are moving to a commune in Taos County, New Mexico, where friends
have preceded them. A typical city couple, they'd
had jobs that were not really meaningful, but that
provided financial means to purchase those things
society says are vital for the good life. Unconvinced
that the acquisition of so many material possessions
was necessary, the McKensies refused to succeed. Instead, they wanted a radical break with the American way; they wanted to return to the land as a
means of rediscovering themselves and of forging a
new life-style. They believed that people who want
to change vast systems must begin the transformation with themselves.

There is no private ownership at the commune, so
the first thing the McKensies must do is to dis-

possess themselves. This process begins with least-needed possessions and becomes more and more difficult as more treasured objects must also be given to the community. All that finally remains is their clothing and their tiny room. Newcomers are to sever themselves from the comforts and the whole pattern of their former affluent life-style so they learn how little it takes to survive. Thoreau's words are often heard in the commune: "A man is rich in proportion to the number of things which he can afford to let alone."

The result is a simple, natural life. Homesteading. Giving up electricity, telephones, running water, washing machines. Creating shelter out of adobe bricks or crude, hand-cut lumber. Building your own cistern.

Anyone who arrives at the commune is welcome and will receive whatever food or shelter the family can provide. However, those who elect to stay must work, either at farming or at construction. Only what can be produced on the land is consumed. Food, clothing, and shelter must all come from available raw materials. There is no tractor. All the farming is done by hand.

Out in the fields, there is only the earth, the cultivators, and God. Here a deep kinship binds the commune members and they satisfy their inner longing for elemental surroundings. Here they feel safe from modern society and the coming 21st century.

Thirty-six Americans, men and women, sit in the lotus posture in a *zendo* in the mountains of California. Most of their time is taken up with "just sitting," or *zazen*, a uniquely Zen form of meditation. *Zazen* is experienced for long periods of time, to learn to face oneself as one really is and to analyze one's reasons for wanting to practice Zen.

The day begins at 4:00 A.M. with the sound of a bronze bell, and then the *han*, an ash plank four inches thick, with a concave surface, is struck with a wooden mallet. Black-robed men and women move quietly along the gravel in the half-light of early morning. There follow alternating periods of *zazen*, eating, and working, with bed at 9:45 P.M. Every minute of the day is scheduled so there may be no lapse from "mindfulness." Mindfulness is to live solely in the present moment, to work totally absorbed in the task at hand, whether driving nails or scrubbing a hardwood floor. This total concentration and attention is a form of meditation peculiar to Zen.

The outdoor *zendo* is set in a breathtakingly beautiful garden. But it is a garden unlike any we may have seen before. Every tree and shrub has been placed with utmost care, evergreens preponderating. But the most interesting feature of the garden is open stretches of sand and gravel, raked in unusual designs. Buried in the sand and gravel are great boulders whose rugged shapes dominate the scene. The whole is backed by a bamboo fence. All materials are natural: wood, stone, gravel, sand, grass, moss, shrubs, trees. What is portrayed here is the world itself, the greater reality in miniature, for all to meditate upon.

Loss of a center

Martin Heidegger described our age as a time of "the no-more of the gods that have fled, and the not-yet of the god that is coming." [1] It is a time between worlds. The world we have known is plainly dying, and it is not yet clear what shape the world being born will take.

About 10 years ago Thomas Altizer and William Hamilton, et al., announced the death of God. That movement, which exploded with so much provocation then, stirs not a ripple today. This is because it was both very right and very wrong. It was right in announcing the widespread decline of belief in the monotheistic God of the Bible. The movement rightly read the secular mood of Western culture, which found much talk about God and about the supernatural world to be empty and meaningless. But it was entirely wrong in failing to recognize that religion was alive and well.

The premature burial of God was soon displaced by spiritual hunger for a new sense of the religious. In a burst of creativity, this hunger turned in all directions, seeking inspiration for a new understanding of human life. One can speak of a religion explosion: Oriental meditation cults, mysticism, magic, the occult! According to a recent Gallup poll, 12% of all Americans practice some mystical discipline. More than 800,000 Transcendental Mediators practice their discipline for 20 minutes faithfully twice a day. This religious explosion has been called a "spiritual revolution" (Jacob Needleman) and even a "new reformation" (Paul Goodman).[2]

Of the many strands producing this movement, two roots can be clearly traced: (1) Interest in Oriental religions was brought home by American servicemen involved in the Pacific theatre in World War II, in the occupation of mainland Japan, and in the Korean War; (2) A profound reaction against the values of modern Western society, in the countercultural movement of the 1960s, led young Americans to seek answers to their religious questions elsewhere than in the traditional religion of their parents.

Because of its centrifugal nature, the resurgence of religion is incredibly complex. It has no single focus, but reaches out in all directions to Oriental

religions, to esoteric tradition, and to modern Western psychotherapy. This centrifugal character provides us with an important clue to its nature.

The truth in the God-is-dead movement of a decade ago is that our traditional monotheistic way of
thinking and speaking about God is meaningful
for fewer and fewer people. We no longer have a
single, integrated center of meaning and moral
values. People no longer believe there is one truth
with a single grammar and logic containing all they
need to know.

Three thousand years ago Moses of Israel taught
that there is no God but one. "I am the Lord your
God. . . . You shall have no other gods before me"
(Exod. 20:2, 3). Only the living God is God, the gods
are nothing but idols, which have no life in them.
The gods are only forces in nature, they are not
divine. Only the God who created nature is divine.
It took centuries, and the active support of some of
Israel's greatest prophets, before monotheism tri-
umphed over polytheism in the West. Much later
this belief in one God and one world created the
climate in which the modern scientific movement
could arise. Nature, like God, was believed to be
singular, which meant the world was unified and
would ultimately yield its secrets to the mind and
science of humanity.

What has happened today is the loss of that center. The experience of people today is not singular,
it is plural. Various ethnic, religious, political, and
cultural ideologies promise meaning simultaneously.
People do not believe that a single system of meaning can explain the breadth of their experience. Contemporary society is so complex, and the roles people
play are so many, that no single center meets their
needs.

What is true in how people find meaning for their

lives is also true of their moral values. Where one scheme of values, e.g., the Ten Commandments, was once considered normative for all persons, and was seen as equally valid at different times and in different situations, people no longer accept that as true. They believe morals depend on the individual and the situation. No truth is true exclusively. Each generation, every religious group, and every subculture within society has its own truth.

With a single center of meaning and moral values gone, the old polytheistic gods are being reborn.[3] In place of the God of Abraham, Isaac, and Jacob, there are many new gods and goddesses; gurus, magicians, and wizards; Transcendental Meditation, the Naropa Institute, Buddhist *zendos;* Theosophy, Gurdjieff, and the human potential movement. The diversity is luxuriant, and any detailed consideration of it is beyond the scope of this book.

However, three major strands disclose themselves. The first group is rooted in ancient Asian religious traditions: Hindu, Buddhist, Zen, and Islamic. A second group is centered in the Western esoteric tradition, having its roots in the polytheism, shamanism, Mithraism, gnosticism, and other religious beliefs of the classical Mediterranean world of 2000 years ago. A third group brings modern psychotherapy into relationship with various Oriental disciplines in what is usually called the human potential movement or sometimes the consciousness revolution.[4]

Groups with Asian religious roots

HINDU   The Ramakrishna Mission and the Vedanta Societies must be credited with introducing Asian religious ideas to the United States just before the end of the 19th century. The Self-

Realization Fellowship of Yogananda and the International Sivananda Yoga Society of Sivananda both concentrate on the practice of yoga, rather than on the more intellectual side of Hinduism. Best known today is the Maharishi Mahesh Yogi's Transcendental Meditation movement, which has swept the United States and given hundreds of thousands of followers a mantra and set them meditating morning and evening. Certainly most colorful have been the members of the International Society for Krishna Consciousness, with their shaved heads, yellow robes, and chants of "Hare Krishna." This movement worships Krishna in the Hindu theistic tradition. The Satya Sai Baba movement centers on a contemporary Indian holy man and healer in South India, and there is Krishnamurti, who was proclaimed a future avatar of the age by the founders of the Theosophical Society. Alongside these movements and individuals, there is the countrywide practice of yoga taught by various television "yogis" and practiced by thousands of individuals for health, therapeutic, and spiritual ends.

BUDDHIST   Buddhism, the great missionary religion of Asia, has made a less obvious, more subtle, impact on Western life. The alternative lifestyles movement of the 1960s, with its communal living and its back-to-nature emphasis, owes much to the Buddhist values of simplification and non-attachment. Buddhism's most influential form is Zen, which we will consider in a grouping of its own. With the conquest of Tibet more than 25 years ago, various Tibetan lamas have come to the United States. Typical centers are the Tibetan Nyingmapa Meditation Center of Rinpoche in Berkeley and the Naropa Institute of Chogyam Trungpa in Boulder. Nichiren Shosho and its lay organization *Soka*

Gakkai, very active in contemporary Japan, have made Western converts.

ZEN BUDDHIST   Zen centers are to be found all over the West today. One of the most famous is the Zen Mountain Center at Tassajara, California. However, it would be a mistake to imply the influence of Zen is limited to these centers. Zen has had a persuasive influence on many American intellectuals, particularly in the universities, and through them on large numbers of young Americans.

ISLAMIC   While groups with Islamic roots cannot claim large numbers of adherents in the West, they are quite fascinating. Baha'i is no newcomer to these shores. Despite its emphasis on the fundamental unity of all religions, it has its roots in the Shiite Islam of Iran. Sufi mysticism is becoming better known as many translations of its literature become available. In the Sufi tradition is Subud, the name of the Indonesian Muslim founder of this movement, which makes experience not unlike that of the "whirling dervishes" available in its *latihan.*

Groups with esoteric tradition roots

The esoteric tradition is a useful designation for a divergence of groups belonging to the alternative-reality tradition in the West, with roots in esoteric Christianity, Kabbalistic and Hasidic Judaism, gnosticism, medieval mysticism, alchemy, etc. Esoteric means hidden or secret, intended only for those few initiated into it. Theosophy, anthroposophy, and Rosicrucianism belong to this group, although they were deeply influenced by the Hindu tradition as well. Spiritualism, with its emphasis on psychic phenomena, belongs to the esoteric tradition. Another group may be termed initiatory, because it in-

volves a master, shaman, or magus who initiates the
disciple into a secret discipline (or *sadhana*). Best
known among this group are the practices associated
with the names of G. I. Gurdjieff and P. D. Ouspen-
sky, and the Scientology of L. Ron Hubbard. Still
another group, which may be termed neopaganism,
includes hundreds of phenomena involving the practice of things such as magic, witchcraft, and Satan-
ism.

Groups with psychotherapeutic roots

One of the newest phenomena is an interesting
meeting of modern, Western psychotherapeutic techniques and various disciplines from Eastern religions. Called the human potential movement by some
and the consciousness revolution by others, the movement is a "spiritual supermarket." [5] Believing that
the new frontier is the world of the inner person,
the practitioners of these remedies want to lead individuals to discover their true potential by throwing
off whatever inhibits them from doing so, such as
society, the family, or traditional religion and morality. Beginning with T groups and encounter groups
of various kinds, the movement has developed into
practices such as EST, biofeedback, Esalen groups,
Arica, and Silva Mind Control, and their many
imitators. A handbook on the consciousness movement numbers 8000 ways to awaken one's potential
in the West today.

Our age, then, has witnessed the loss of a single,
integrated center of meaning, synonymous in the
West with worship of the one God of the Bible, and a
unified scheme of moral values based on that same
Bible. In place of the one, we now have the many,
a parade of gods and goddesses bewildering to the
most unruffled observer. It would take a much

bigger book to deal with even the main features of these three strands of the resurgence of religion in our time. The range of this study is narrowed to the impact of the religions of Asia on modern, Western society. Since the homeland of Islam is not properly Oriental, but rather Middle Eastern, it is excluded from the study, and we will concentrate on the Hindu, the Theravada Buddhist, and the Zen Buddhist traditions.

The advent of science, and a universe devoid of meaning

Not only are modern Westerners experiencing the loss of a center, they are also *turning inward*. All people have both an inner and an outer world, and their most essential task is bringing meaning into both. At any given point in history, one of these worlds must make sense if human life is to be nurtured. During many epochs of history, the outer, cultural world provided a sense of wholeness, a sense of meaning. But the fabric of this one world was broken once and for all with the advent of empirical science and the modern age. The structure of human life, built on a foundation of accepted values and meanings, was fragmented beyond recovery. The accepted religious understanding of the universe, with the earth at its center, with humanity as its purpose, and with God present as its creator and sustainer, was questioned and discarded.

In ancient times people believed that God or the gods were intimately involved in the operation of natural processes. The name for this way of understanding the world is *animism*. In fact, it is the oldest form of religion about which we know. Animism was ancient humanity's science, its rudimentary way of understanding nature and how it worked. What impressed early humans most was that living bodies breathed and dead ones did not. They reasoned that breath animated the body, gave it life, and made it move. In many traditional languages the same word is used for the closely related concepts of breath and spirit. From this, early humans inferred that nature was alive with spirit. When clouds moved across the sky, it was the spirits of the clouds that moved them. Since the sun rose daily in the east and set in the west, and stars and planets changed their positions in the night sky, the spirits of the sun, stars, and planets must move them through the sky. The germination of seed and the flow of great rivers was explained in the same way.

All higher religions have come out of such animism. In the Middle East, Judaism, Christianity, and Islam were radically monotheistic, so there could be no talk of spirits or gods animating nature. However, there was no reason why the one God, Lord of heaven and earth, could not be understood in this way. This family of religions taught that God was not only the creator of nature, but also its sustainer and provider. He was the giver of new life, present in the germinating of the seed, in the life-giving rainfall, in the harvest, in the changing seasons.

This understanding of nature survived intact until the rise of science in the 17th and 18th centuries. Science did not set out to undermine the authority of religion, but it discovered and described how nature worked without using the activity of God as explanation. It soon became clear that God did not literally move clouds across the sky, set planets in their orbit, cause seeds to germinate, make it rain. All of these processes could be explained naturally. The unintended effect of the new science was to render God unemployed.

More important still, the universe was emptied of

its spirit. It came to be understood as a vast, complicated machine. Like a machine, it operated very nicely on its own, according to scientific laws, without any help from a divine spirit. And since the design of the world is the work of the divine spirit, eventually any sense of meaning or purpose was declared absent from the machine. It was just there. In this way modern science became materialistic in its view of the universe and used a mechanistic model to explain its operation. Materialism was the counterpart to denying that a divine spirit dwelled in the universe, and the mechanistic model was a way of saying the universe operated independently.

This view of the universe may be helpful to the scientist, but it is devastating to humanity's sense of its place in the world. A mechanical universe is blind, devoid of purpose. How does humanity fit into that kind of world? Given that model, human life is an accidental product of biological evolution, resident in a universe which cannot and does not care whether it lives or dies. Human life appears like a tiny oasis of meaning and caring in the purposelessness of vast empty space.

This analysis provides us with an important clue for understanding our present religious situation. Unable to point to meaning in the universe any longer because of the overwhelming authority of modern science, people have turned away from such a view with a shudder and looked for meaning in the depths of their inner world. Remarkably, they have discovered that the world can be understood inside-out as profoundly as it can be understood outside-in.

As different as they are from one another in other ways, the many groups involved in the resurgence of religion join in using their world within as a model for the world without. The human world within is devoid of neither spirit nor meaning, nor does it function like a machine. It is rich in spiritual potential and in meaning and purpose. It is vital, growing, and alive.

When applied to the world without, this provides an organismic rather than mechanical model of the universe. Adherents to this view argue that the universe is not particularly like a machine. The universe both reproduces and evolves. No machine, however complicated, can reproduce, creating new machines, nor can it evolve into a different kind of machine. That is because a machine is not alive—but the universe is alive. According to the new consciousness, the machine model of the universe should be replaced with the model of an organism.

The resurgence of religion is a reaction against the age of science and its view of the universe. Its alternative view sees everything that exists as interrelated. The world is one and whole and humanity belongs to that wholeness as a significant part. The life of the human individual is not arbitrary and solitary, but part of a larger purpose and greater unity.

This great affirmation finds all the "new religions" together turning inward, away from an outer world devoid of meaning to a world rich in human promise and creativity. Unable to make meaningful the outer world of modern science, they have turned their inner world inside out and are viewing the larger universe as organismic and whole.

Modern industrial society and the dehumanizing of humanity

Another cause of the *turn inward* is the inability of modern industrial society to meet the human need for meaning and hope.

The advent of modern science, which promised the

liberation of humanity, produced technology. And technology, the world of the machine, has created a standard of living our forebearers, even a few generations ago, could not have imagined. But like modern science itself, technology has proved to be a mixed blessing. The machine has made life much easier for people, but it has also proved a significant challenge to their humanity. In a surprising way the machine, designed to serve people, has threatened to become their master. Labor is performed in many cases more efficiently and more perfectly by the machine.

The great dream of the industrial revolution was that technical achievement would mean economic growth, and that the product of both would be human progress and a perpetually rising standard of living. The exhaustion of that dream and its inability to satisfy the human spirit has caused many people to turn for meaning from the outer world of industry and commerce to inner states of experience.

The drive for wealth and power, the profit motive, has fueled the astounding growth of the modern industrial world. But affluence cannot buy meaning for life. The obsession with material production leaves little time or place for cultivating personal human values.

The countercultural movement of the 1960s exploded upon the American scene, witnessing to a massive erosion of the legitimacy of this mentality and of American institutions generally. Many young Americans questioned or repudiated the work ethic and the profit motive. It appeared to them that the quest for wealth and power was destroying the quality and meaning of life.

There were two sides to the movement, one which sought *alternative politics,* and another which sought *alternative life-styles.*[6] The first was made up of political activists intent upon overthrowing the present social and political system in order to create a more humane society. The other turned away from the world in order to embody a new life-style within.

> The difference between demonstrations and sit-ins on the one hand and love-ins, be-ins, and rock festivals on the other illustrates the contrast.[7]

The day of those who wanted significant social and political change has come and gone. However, the movement for alternative life-styles has not only persisted, it shows signs of sustained momentum. Both groups were deeply critical of contemporary American society, but those who wanted to overthrow the present social and political system became increasingly doctrinaire and were dominated by the work ethic, very like the order they wanted to overthrow. By contrast, those experimenting with alternative life-styles tried to create and embody a new way of life, while still remaining part of the old society. Despairing of the external world, these "flower children" turned inward for meaning through drugs, music, and meditation.

Asian spirituality was in stark contrast to the mentality of the established order and therefore provided an ideal form for reaction against it. Where modern Western society emphasized external achievement, exploitation of natural resources, and impersonal technology, the new mood stressed inner experience, harmony with nature and the natural dimensions of life, and intimate personal relationships of the deepest sort. The new mood rejected hard work, competition, careerism, status seeking, and the sacrifice of present fulfillment for some future goal. All of these belonged to the established order. In their place were valued small-scale production of handicrafts, farming, small face-to-face communities often on a communal pattern, and simplicity and naturalness in food and clothing.[8] People were urged to look to themselves, to turn inward, and to discover within themselves the meaning for life denied them in the world outside.

So, on the one hand, modern science, with its new understanding of the universe, undermined the traditional meaning of human life, and, on the other hand, technology attacked men and women's very usefulness by performing many of their functions better than they could perform them themselves. It is easy to understand why people turned inward. But mainline Christianity was not particularly congenial to the turn inward, whereas concentration on inner experience has been a part of the genius of Asian religions for centuries. Rich in techniques for laying open the depths of the self, they were ideally suited for the historical situation in which Westerners found themselves. Yoga and meditation, development of the "mind," higher states of consciousness, filled a void in Western humanity's experience and operated in defense of its humanity in the scientific age.

Chapter 2

What attracts Westerners to Eastern religions?

What strikes the observer about the resurgence of religion is its complexity. Chapter 1 distinguished three major strands of the resurgence, one of which provides the focus of this book. This chapter analyzes 11 features of attraction Eastern religions have for Westerners.

1. A unitary view of the world

A little more than 100 years ago, the Theosophical Society was one of the first to introduce the pantheism of India to the West. In its lecture halls and through its many publications, it spoke of realizing the fundamental oneness underlying all things. The world is not many, nor two, but one. The underlying unity of all that exists is reflected in the presence of the divine world-soul throughout the universe.

From the Greeks, Westerners inherited a two-world concept: the natural, earthly world, and, mirroring it, a supernatural, transcendent world. During the Middle Ages these worlds were thought of as the "this-worldly," or secular, and the "other-worldly," or sacred.

The great difficulty with this two-world concept

is that it permits the modern interpretation of the earthly world operating solely by natural causes which the scientist can measure and study, while the transcendent world is seen as moved by supernatural or spiritual forces belonging to the realm of being above and beyond that which science can study and measure. This has led our age to teach that only this earthly world, the existence of which can be proven scientifically, is real.

Whatever belongs to that supernatural world, then—God, spiritual realities, and moral values—is unreal according to the modern scientific worldview. Not only does this point of view foster modern atheism, but it empties the universe of all spiritual and moral values. Humanity is left frighteningly alone in a vast universe that dwarfs it, that surrounds it on every side, and that it cannot comprehend.

In the resurgence of religion, this two-world conception of the universe is discarded. Adherents believe that there is one world, not two, and that a divine presence, and the presence of spiritual and moral values, pervade every corner of the universe. In this more unitary view of the universe, there is no separation of worlds: the divine presence, humanity, spiritual and moral values are all closely interrelated. In this way a significant step is taken toward putting back together the fragmented 20th-century world.

The oneness of God and his world is beautifully captured in the often-quoted words of the *Maitri Upanishad* 6:17:

> In the beginning all was God (Brahman), One and infinite. He is beyond north and south, and east and west, and beyond what is above or below. His infinity is everywhere. In him there is neither above, nor across, nor below; and in him there is neither east nor west.

The Spirit supreme is immeasurable, inapprehensible, beyond conception, never-born, beyond reasoning, beyond thought. His vastness is the vastness of space.

At the end of the worlds, all things sleep: he alone is awake in Eternity. Then from his infinite space new worlds arise and awake, a universe which is a vastness of thought. In the consciousness of God (Brahman) the universe is, and into him it returns.

He is seen in the radiance of the sun in the sky, in the brightness of fire on earth, and in the fire of life that burns the food of life. Therefore it has been said:

He who is in the sun, and in the fire and in the heart of man is ONE. He who knows this is one with the ONE.[1]

At its best, then, this view of the world does not separate the spiritual and the earthly. It views them as intimately interrelated in the same sphere of existence. By making a fragmented and divided world one again, it serves an important religious purpose. The universe is no longer empty and meaningless, because the divine, the spiritual, and the moral permeate the whole. The difference is between a deserted world and an inhabited one. The Eastern religions find their view to be the best way of constructing and sustaining a rich religious worldview amid the secularism of the modern age.

2. A mystical relationship with the world

A group of disciples of a Tibetan Buddhist *roshi* sit quietly before a *thanka* or *mandala,* a picture-chart used as a focus for meditation. The chart symbolizes the integration of all reality. A Buddha figure, seated in profound meditation, is surrounded by concentric circles filled with the material elements of the world and all the deities and creatures of the cosmos in rings of descending significance. By meditation, the disciples join in the unity the chart portrays.

If a one-world concept gives unity to reality, mysticism is the direct, firsthand communion of the individual person with the divine presence in the universe. The experience of the sacred lies at the root of all religion. In discovering this sacred presence, and in entering into relationship with it, people may see their true being for the first time. Finding this spiritual dimension in the universe and finding one's own spiritual dimension are indistinguishable for the mystic. The *Chandogya Upanishad* 3:14 says:

> There is a Spirit that is mind and life, light and truth and vast spaces. . . . He enfolds the whole universe, and in silence is loving to all.
> This is the Spirit that is in my heart, smaller than a grain of rice, or a grain of barley, or a grain of mustard-seed, or a grain of canary seed, or the kernel of a grain of canary-seed. This is the Spirit that is in my heart, greater than the earth, greater than the sky, greater than heaven itself, greater than all these worlds.[2]

The mystical experience yields insight into depths of truth denied the intellect. It is not the truth of reason or the truth of Holy Scripture. It is the mystic's inner truth. It defies expression and it cannot be conveyed in words. It must be directly experienced in itself. It cannot be communicated or imparted to another.[3]

Such mystical experience is the counterpart to having a unified view of the world. Mystics experience a sense of wholeness, a sense of belonging, a sense of being an organic part of the greater world. They are aware of overcoming any alienation, any sense of distance between themselves and their world. They are no longer strangers. All things lose distinctness. And in this experience of unity and integration, there is great personal strength. The final outcome, all mystics report, is great serenity. Just as a one-world conception helps people put the fragmented nature of the world back together into a single, integrated whole, so mysticism helps them integrate themselves with the spiritual presence surrounding them. Instead of feeling like alienated outcasts in the universe, they feel that they belong, that they are at home.

3. Freedom from modern Western materialism

The new communes scattered throughout the Western world pursue a very old ideal: abandoning materialism for a community organized around more satisfying goals. The commune is a family, living simply, withdrawn from society, united by its pursuit of contemplation, experiencing wholeness in its harmony with the natural world.

The materialism of modern Western society has spawned its own reaction. The emphasis on personal achievement and on the acquisition of material possessions stifles the human spirit. Preoccupation with the marketplace, production, profits, and the accumulation and manipulation of capital cannot give meaning to a person's life. More and more people caught up in the business affairs and competition of modern life tire of this exhausting treadmill and would like nothing more than to escape it.

But Westerners find it very difficult to escape because of the nature of their consuming society. People have to buy more and more goods and services to keep the economy growing, so the business community must find ways to escalate people's needs. And the more complicated their needs, the more firmly they are bound to the system supplying them.

The only way out of this dilemma is to de-escalate

one's needs. This frees one from the thralldom of material possessions and from dependency on the products manufactured by society. Westerners are declaring their freedom from materialism in various ways in the resurgence of religion. Many groups teach their adherents to recognize the relative unimportance of the material side of life and to live for spiritual values instead. These people remain within society, but are not caught up in the compulsion to consume.

An increasing number of people have joined religious groups to which they make significant financial commitments as a way to reduce their reliance on the material, and some have joined communal groups requiring them to share all their worldly goods with the community. A recent Harris poll found a major shift already underway—some five to ten million Americans are adopting a life-style of increasing "voluntary simplicity." In all of this there is much searching, however imperfect, for meaningful ways of liberation from the oppressive materialism of technological society. Such experimentation is likely to continue.

4. Many paths to the truth

Humanity cannot live without a center. On every hand people of the 20th century are trying to create unity in their fragmented lives. But in a pluralistic society, that is very difficult. The result is an odd mingling of primitive magic, profound Oriental philosophy, astrology, yogic methods, and many other elements. Let each person create a personal mosaic of meaning out of these ingredients.

In the West truth is singular. There has been a sense of theological rightness, resting on the belief that in the Word of God Christians possess the single

truth. The new religious consciousness leans instead
to the Asian conception of truth. In India the truth
has many names. There are as many paths to the
truth as there are seekers on the way. In a very
tolerant way, Hindus and Buddhists believe everyone
has a part of the truth, however rudimentary, and
should be encouraged to follow that truth in con-
fidence that it will lead finally to higher truth.

People belonging to the resurgence in religion in
the West today are very suspicious of the concept of
one truth and reluctant to accept what they see as
the verbal and intellectual nature of mainline Christianity. They find the latter exclusive, while they
want to include truth from whatever source it may
come. In its astounding complexity, the movement
borrows truths from the most diverse sources. It
does not matter what the sources are, as long as
these features contribute to a range of experience
the individual finds meaningful. It is not uncommon
to find understandings and practices from Zen Buddhist, esoteric Christian, Hindu, primitive magic,
and astrological sources side by side in a loose blending. So long as they meet the individual's needs,
their labels do not matter.

The counterpart to this attitude is a certain am-
biguity and imprecision about the blending of these
understandings and practices. It is not important
that they should be a logical whole, so long as they
meet the individual's needs. In fact, there is a de-
liberate unwillingness to draw out the logical consequences of a position, lest it conflict with other
convictions held by the same individual.

There is, in addition, a broad tolerance of views.
Quite literally anything may be accepted, even elements that might otherwise have been considered
superstitious or unworthy. Nothing is to be despised,
even tarot cards or numerology, if it is meaningful

to the individual. This eclecticism, this indiscriminate blending of usages, and this broad tolerance run contrary to the dominant Western mentality, which holds its truth to be singular and superior to all other expressions of truth.

5. The promise of altering human consciousness

The human potential movement, combining psychotherapy and Oriental meditation skills, seeks to tap the roots of the individual's potential and to help the person realize that potential. At the Esalen Institute, for example, people are led to abandon all fixed views of themselves, inherited moral values, and habits of behavior. In this way individuals reach beyond societal strictures to their own potential, and they set out on a road of making and remaking themselves.

People who exhibit the new mood in Western religious life today are looking for the prospect of inner transformation. They insist that religion be experiential and that it offer them a specific spiritual path or discipline. They are looking for self-realization, in a time of rapid and threatening change in the external world. They are seeking religious forms that exhibit transforming power. Because they believe traditional forms of Western religious life have lost their power to transform, they are looking for new forms. These people want to enter, or are fascinated by the possibility of entering, an advanced, ecstatic state of consciousness. They desire altered states of consciousness, because they want to transcend ordinary, everyday experience.

Those who focus on inner experience challenge competition and success in the outer world as the proper purpose for a human life. Key terms are *altered consciousness, inner awareness, potential, ful-*

fillment. People desire an intensity of experience on the frontiers of the inner world. This is because they are convinced that the world perceived by ordinary, everyday awareness is inferior to the world disclosed by an expanding consciousness. They believe they can change their lives by widening the spectrum of their consciousness and thereby putting themselves in touch with a higher reality.

Many people feel that something is missing in their lives and they want to tap an inner potential of self-development. The development of their potential appears to be their most fundamental personal task. They are convinced such development will put them in better touch with themselves, with others, with nature, and with the forces of the cosmos. However differently these forces are defined, as supernatural or magical or divine, the faith is strong that they can help the individual in self-development, if only he or she can be put in touch with them.

Behind this desire for altered consciousness and development in inner awareness is a new vision of the possibilities open for humanity. In a way that is very Western, there is strong belief in what another generation called the innate goodness of humanity. Westerners have traditionally been optimistic about humanity's future and particularly about the promise of change to better the human situation. These traditional Western themes now support people's faith in the inherent alterability of human character. Where a decade or two ago people may have pursued peace of mind or Norman Vincent Peale's power of positive thinking, today they want to realize higher states of consciousness.

Such people want inner transformation and they are very impatient with words, with religious dialog or instruction that does not lead directly to it.

They find the Buddha's approach to this need to be very congenial. Like him they are intensely practical. The Buddha refused to indulge in religious or metaphysical speculation that could not be related directly to the human need for change he saw in those who came to him. In one of his best-known similes he said:

> Should anyone say: I am not willing to lead the disciples' life under the Perfect One unless the Perfect One first tells me whether the world is eternal or temporal; whether the world is finite or infinite; whether the personality is identical with the body, or whether the personality is one thing and the body another; whether the Perfect One continues to exist after death, such a one, Brothers, would die ere the Perfect One could tell him all this.
>
> It is, Brothers, as if a man were pierced through by a poisoned arrow, and his friends, companions, and near relatives called in a surgeon, and he should say, "I will not have this arrow pulled out until I know who the man is that has wounded me; whether he is of the royal caste or the priest's caste, a citizen or a servant;" or else he should say, "I will not have this arrow pulled out until I know who the man is that has wounded me; what is his name and to what family he belongs;" or else he should say, "I will not have this arrow pulled out until I know who the man is that has wounded me, whether he is tall or short, or of medium height;" verily, Brothers, such a one would die ere he could sufficiently get to know all this (*Anguttara-Nikaya*).[4]

6. Direct rather than secondary experience

Young devotees, dressed in yellow robes, their heads shaved, dance and chant "Hare Krishna" on the walks of a college campus. They are clearly lost in their rapture, carried away by the orgiastic intensity of their experience. They are filled with love and devotion for Lord Krishna, himself the Hindu avatar of God as love. So great is Krishna's passion

for the human soul, and so intense the human response, that the telling of it is a divine-human love
story.

Those attracted by Asian religions want direct
experience of religious reality and are impatient
with the Western verbal tradition. They want to discover what is religiously real in their own experience; there will be time to describe it in words and
ideas later. The experience this new mood is seeking
is nonverbal. The great medieval mystics of the
West called it *via negativa*, the negative way. They
meant their experience could not be analyzed or
thought about by the mind and that it could not be
described in words. The technical term for this kind
of experience is *ineffable* (inexpressible or inde-
scribable). Western adherents to Eastern religions
criticize Christian forms as excessively verbal and
failing to touch the center of human existence.
Words are merely symbols for facts and experiences,
and therefore an indirect approach to truth. What
these people desire is a direct, spontaneous, and in-
tuitive experience of truth, without verbal inter-
mediacies.

In fact, one may speak of a cult of experience.
Central to this cult is emphasis on the present
moment, on the here and now. Contemporary Westerners do not value the history or traditions of religions, however rich and interesting they may be.
The traditions on which Western civilization is
based no longer seem to embody the resources for
creating meaning in life. Rather than revere the
past, people are looking to present experience for
whatever meaning there is.

The contemporary mood is unwilling to labor for
future rewards; it desires gratification and satisfaction in the present. Neither past nor future holds
life's meaning. Responsiveness, genuineness, and

spontaneity in the present moment are the new values. The meaning of life will be found within the self and within its experience in the here and now.[5]

These people are more comfortable with the view of authority taught by Buddhism than with that of the Middle Eastern religions. Very simply, the Buddha urged his followers to test their religious insights in their own experience and to accept no other authority than that test. This advice is unique in the history of religions:

> Do not be led by reports, or traditions, or hearsay. Be not led by the authority of religious texts, nor by mere logic or inference . . . but . . . when you know for yourselves that certain things are unwholesome, and wrong, and bad, then give them up. . . . And when you know for yourselves that certain things are wholesome and good, then accept them and follow them (*Anguttara-Nikaya*).[6]

The Buddha went even further. He told his followers they should test the Buddha himself, to prove his teachings in their own experience.[7] The only religion that can serve people's needs is that which they make their own. This is exactly what adherents of the Eastern religions believe. Whatever cannot prove itself in their experience is of no interest to them.

7. A specific program of spiritual discipline

When many people think of spiritual discipline, they imagine a recluse sitting cross-legged, meditating quietly in a cave in some remote corner of the world. In the place of such passivity, life in a Zen monastery is strenuously disciplined. Every moment of the day is regulated: work alternates with *zazen* (sitting meditation), and study with food and sleep. The discipline becomes the vehicle of liberation.

Direct religious experience is not likely to occur by chance without religious discipline. Between the diagnosis of what is wrong with humanity and our hope for what it may become, there must exist a bridge. This bridge is the discipline, method, or technique by which religion brings about an inner transformation.[8] The Eastern religions which are attracting so much attention in the West stress the importance of religious discipline. That is why we hear so much about techniques of meditation, yoga, mantras, and *zazen.*

The contemporary resurgence of religion turns to its Oriental roots for a *sadhana,* a spiritual exercise or path by which an individual awakens to full consciousness. To be effective it must be a specific and concrete program for spiritual growth, with carefully defined and attainable goals.

So many religious ideals are lofty, abstract, remote, and difficult to attain. If the ideals are set too high, the individual will strive for a time to attain them and then grow discouraged and abandon the struggle. If the ideals are generalized and vague, the individual will have great difficulty applying them in everyday situations. So much religious moralizing is of this kind, impractically idealistic and lacking in concreteness.

Those influenced by Eastern religions are painfully aware of this common failing of much Western religious teaching. For this condition, a spiritual discipline is an effective antidote. Such a path is usually undertaken with the guidance of a master, a guru or *roshi,* who prescribes for the individual's specific needs. Then, if the discipline is followed faithfully, it will lead to decided and significant changes in the person's spiritual condition.

It seems ironic today that the Christian community has gradually been discarding practices that represent the discipline of the Christian life (e.g., Lenten practices). It has been doing so ever since the end of the medieval world in the Protestant Reformation of the 16th century. Oriental criticism of Western spirituality centers on the fact that only in the West are people without a *sadhana,* a carefully plotted spiritual path. Christians have wanted to emphasize the grace of God and have done so at the cost of religious discipline. A highly disciplined religious path may also appear to some to be a denial of the individual freedom Westerners prize so much. Whatever the reasons may be, there is in this permissive time a longing for spiritual discipline and for what it accomplishes. Yoga and meditation, restricted diet and fasting, withdrawal from society, and a vow of silence are solitary pursuits, but highly disciplined ones that appear to meet the need of the hour.

8. Prayer becomes meditative and contemplative

Wishing to meditate, the Transcendental Meditation initiate closes his eyes halfway and repeats his *mantra* silently to himself. The *mantra* is a Sanskrit word or phrase that focuses the mind away from worldly distractions. The vibrations of its sound effectively shut out all other sense experiences. The mind comes to rest, and the meditator experiences great serenity.

There is no better clue to the meaning of the current resurgence of religion than its pursuit of meditation and other mystical skills. So little emphasis is put on discipline of the mind and spirit in the West, it is difficult for us to understand the importance placed on it in Asia. Part of the reason is a lack of understanding. When Westerners think about meditation they typically conceive of someone sitting passively in a stylized posture, caught up in some kind of mysterious trance. This caricature misses the point. What is happening has little to do with the outward form, posture, or mantras. The important thing is a particular *quality* of experience.

Although what follows puts the matter in Western terms, it can nevertheless help us understand the difference between prayer and meditation. At the root of it, there are only two fundamentally different ways of understanding the relationship between God and his world. In the first, God occupies a world above and beyond the present one. Looking down from his dwelling place above, God brought this world into being, peopled it with men and women, and controls their destinies rather like a master puppeteer. For those who accept this analogy, prayer is largely getting on good terms with this all-powerful deity, begging his forgiveness, and asking his all-powerful help with problems and difficulties beyond the ability of the individual to solve. The appropriate form of prayer for this kind of relationship is petition. The worshiper implores God's intervention into this world from outside it to help with some problem or need.

In the other understanding of the relationship between God and the universe, God is not distinct from the world or at some remote distance from it. God is the divine life, the creativity at the root of this world, from which it draws its life. God is thus not an agent, a divine person out in space somewhere, but a presence to be discovered in the depths of an individual's experience. The divine is not distant, it is closer than one is to oneself. Coming into relationship with the divine, then, is not relating as one person to another, but rather overcoming alienation from a presence at the roots of one's own life. When the relationship is defined this way, the appropriate form of prayer is not petition, but meditation and contemplation of the divine reality underlying all of life.

While not every practitioner of yoga or meditation defines the practice in precisely these terms, most speak of inner peace, wholeness, and overcoming alienation from oneself, from others, from nature, and from the cosmic forces in the universe.

9. Cultivating the bodily dimension of life

The *yogi* combines diet, deep breathing, and discipline of posture to bring spiritual liberation. In *kundalini yoga* the goal is to withdraw life energy from the outer world and focus it within. The *yogic* practice is designed to bring psychic power from the *cakra*, at the base of the spine, up through various spiritual centers to the mind, where it can free the spirit.

Just as adherents to these new religious practices are unwilling to recognize any distance between the self and the divine presence in the world, so are they unwilling to recognize any distance between spirit and body. An organismic view of the cosmos requires an organismic view of the human person.

From the Greeks, Westerners inherited a view of the human being which stressed the dual nature in spirit and body, and which taught that spirit represents humanity's higher nature. Humanity's spirit is like the divine in it, while its body belongs to the earth and its animal past. This led, understandably, to a denigration of the body and everything belonging to it, the commonplace and everyday side of life. People spoke about conquering the body and cultivating the spirit.

Today the newer forms of religion view the human being in an entirely different way. For them there is no duality, but a unity of soul and body, a psychosomatic unity. The human being is an organic whole, with all of its functions intimately inter-related. The only life the spirit can know is in the body. Nothing can happen to one part of the or-ganism without influencing the whole.

An important reason Eastern religious practices are succeeding in the West is their ability to pre-scribe for the human body as well as the human mind. Among the prescriptions are yoga and medita-tion, diet and fasting. The philosophy behind the practice of yoga is the best key to understanding this emphasis. Yoga is a set of practices taking place on many different levels. The preliminaries involve carefully prescribed *asanas* or bodily postures aimed at discipline of bodily movement, muscle, and nerve. The more advanced *asanas* involve considerable agility and skill, and can only be accomplished by careful practice over a long period of time. How-ever, self-control of posture and breathing is not an end in itself. The real goal of yoga is to attain such discipline of the body that one can undertake dis-cipline of mind and spirit. Yogis have taught for centuries that no one can undertake the very difficult task of controlling mind and spirit before disciplin-ing the body. By proceeding in this way, the re-ligions of Asia speak to the whole person as a unity of body and spirit.

10. A guide to the realm of the spirit

The labyrinth of the inner world is so complex, wise is the person who does not travel there alone. What is needed is esoteric (hidden) wisdom. Such wisdom is precious; it has been acquired by the guru by costly experience. The guru is, as a result, a seer who "sees" more deeply into the meaning of the inner world and has experienced it more richly than others. Fortunate is the disciple who is initiated into such wisdom.

Most Eastern religions teach that spiritual progress is impossible without a master, a guru or *roshi*. In fact, the greatest care is taken in Asia in selecting the right teacher and in establishing a lasting relationship with him. The relationship founded between him and his students is often so deep that Indians venerate their gurus in the same way as they do their fathers and mothers.

In the West today the religious groups whose inspiration is Oriental are also directed by unusual, charismatic leaders. Such masters offer initiation *(diksha)* to their disciples into the realm of spiritual mysteries. As a person may gather maps and good advice about alternative routes for a trip to a part of the country he has never visited before, so the disciple needs direction before embarking on travel in the world of inner space. The guru is one who has traveled widely in that inner world.

In return for the guru's help, the student *(shishya)* gives the teacher utmost reverence, cares for his needs, and obeys his commands implicitly. It is not too much to say that the relationship demands complete surrender of the disciple's will. It is a master-apprentice relationship, but one with special intimacy, because it is also viewed as therapeutic. Modern psychotherapy is a relative newcomer to human history. For centuries, in Asia, the relationship with a guru was one of the few therapeutic means available.

In the West, people have grown accustomed to another conception of religious leadership. Their religion centers in an *emissary* prophet (Max Weber's distinction) who speaks on behalf of God and in his name makes ethical demands on his hearers. In the East no prophet comes demanding social justice.

Instead the typical religious leader is *exemplary*. In other words, he is a charismatic personality who does not so much deliver a message on God's behalf as illustrate a life-style others can readily follow.

The charismatic leader of the Asian religious group in this country personifies a particular spiritual path. He is, in fact, its embodiment, illustrating its methods and its goals in his life. It is this living embodiment of the spiritual path, close enough to be observed and imitated by the devotee's own life, that sets Eastern religions apart from what Westerners ordinarily encounter in their churches.

In a time of widespread disillusionment with the traditional forms of Western religious life, people are falling under the influence of dominating religious leaders of this kind. In times of disillusionment, the appeal of turning over one's destiny to someone who has the truth can be overwhelming. Acceptance of such an authoritative figure holds much promise, and also much danger.

11. Living harmoniously with nature

In the great tradition of Chinese and Japanese landscape painting, nature is not used as a backdrop for human subjects. Instead, nature is the subject, and the viewer searches with difficulty for some evidence of human life. Nature is the whole; people are merely parts of that greater sum. To understand the relationship between the whole and the parts is to discover the deeper harmony.

One mark of the current Oriental mood is longing for harmony with nature. Behind this longing lies a fundamental difference between Eastern and Western conceptions of time. The Asian's cyclical view of time is the older of the two. Ultimately it is drawn from the cycle of nature. Spring arises fresh with fragile new life after the barren winter. The summer heat follows, and all growing things come to their maturity. Then autumn begins its gradual decline. Finally the winter winds and cold bring death. All life is enshrouded until the coming of spring, when the whole cycle begins anew. The Eastern view of time and history is modeled on this cycle. History is viewed as eternal recurrence, without beginning and without end, without evolution or progress.

The linear view of time is the product of the great prophets of Israel. They believed that history had its beginning in the creative act of God, and that it would have its end in God's judgment. Between beginning and end, every human being has one lifetime in which to choose decisively the kind of person to be and the kind of life to lead, in correspondence with or in opposition to the will of God. One lifetime, and then the judgment, as history moves toward its end.

Adherents of Eastern religions in the West today are drawn to a cyclical view of time and to harmony with the natural order as a great source of personal strength. They believe such harmony restores humanity to its rightful place in nature once again.

The 20th century, scarred by the horror of two world wars, has had a "terrifying experience of historical time." [9] People want to deny that terror. They do not wish to live in an historical world in which such radical change is occuring. Therefore they want to abandon the realm of history and retreat into a natural paradise beyond history's reach. This longing to return to Eden is a new theme in the West.

There is another reason for this deep-seated desire. It is a reaction against the victimization of this planet and its resources by modern technological society. Westerners have made the world of nature

a workshop. Plants and animals, minerals and resources, are there to be used as tools for humanity.
The industrial revolution has given us the power to
largely mold and remake nature according to our
plan. But this technological revolution has also
scarred the earth, exhausted its resources, and left
blight in its path.

There is nostalgia for unspoiled nature, as it was
before humanity put it to its own selfish purposes.
As a reaction to technological society, nature's
sacredness is being rediscovered. It is no longer being seen as lifeless or subhuman, readily disposable
or usable, existing solely to serve human needs. Instead it is viewed as the rich, fertile environment in
which all forms of life are rooted. To shorten its life
is to shorten human life on this planet. Questing for
a lost human identity, many have found the answer
in union of the human self and the nature that has
produced it. They have rediscovered humanity as belonging to the natural world and cooperating with
its tides and rhythms: the points of the compass,
the changing seasons, the orbits of the heavenly
bodies.

Either humanity is an accident in the universe,
and therefore alone in a scheme of things that does
not and cannot care whether it lives or dies, or
humanity belongs to the natural order of things
and has a proper place in it. In the first case people
are aliens and strangers, in the second the earth is
their home and they belong to it. Western adherents
of Eastern religions have chosen the latter view, and
their conception of humanity in nature has proved
to be a great source of strength to them.

These are the major features attracting Westerners to Eastern religions. Chapter 3 traces the
sources of these features in the Hindu tradition,

Chapter 4 in the Theravada Buddhist tradition, and Chapter 5 in the tradition of Zen Buddhism. Chapter 6 analyzes some concerns Christians have about these 11 features of Eastern religions, and Chapter 7 suggests some things Christians may learn from them.

Chapter 3

Sources in
the classical Hindu tradition

While the Transcendental Meditation into which Craig was initiated in Chapter 1 was brought to the United States for the first time in 1959 by the Maharishi Mahesh Yogi, the heritage out of which it comes is as old as India itself. However successful the packaging of his product for the American market, the Maharishi had for 14 years been the disciple of Swami Brahmananda Saraswati, the leader of one of India's most venerable monasteries, founded by the great Sankara in the ninth century. Sankara was the formulator of Vedanta, "the end of the Vedas," in its classical form. The end of the Vedas are the *Upanishads,* the second great body of Indian scriptures. They comprise the classical tradition that has produced the characteristic features of Hinduism most attractive to Westerners.

Classical Hinduism addresses the basic questions of human life in a manner so different from that of Westerners that it will be necessary to learn a brief vocabulary if we are to understand it.

Atman is a primary term meaning "breath" and therefore "soul" or "spirit." Ancient peoples believed breath or spirit to be a divine substance that brought

life and that literally animated beings in nature to
perform their functions.

This was a very common view. What was uncommon about Hindu thinking was that the *atman* was
viewed as eternal, the one unchanging essence within
a world of continual change.

In its changelessness the *atman* is part of a
greater reality. Everything that exists has an *atman*
and, like all other spirits, is a fragment of the cosmic
atman. Just as individual beings are animated by
atmans, the universe has breath or spirit filling it.
This World-Spirit is called *Brahman.*

Brahman is the highest reality, the spirit within
and beyond the world of time and space. *Brahman* is
alone real, changeless in a world of change, and
therefore always contrasted with the world of time
and space, called *maya*. The changing world of time
and space, *maya,* has changeless *Brahman* as its
source and foundation. *Brahman* brings the world
of *maya* into being, is its "life," and finally reabsorbs
it into itself.

All beings pass through this world of time and
space, having come from *Brahman* and certain to
return to *Brahman*. Between beginning and end, the
atman must wander, passing from one existence to
another. This wandering is termed *samsara,* "trans-
migration of souls." Each rebirth of the *atman* is
determined by the law of *karma*. *Karma* is the law
of absolute cause and effect. *Karma* dictates that the
effects will follow with absolute certainty from their
causes. No good thought or action will fail to have its
consequence.

The goal of Hinduism is to stop the cycle of re-
births, to which people are bound, by coming to
nirvana. So long as they are engrossed in the world
of *maya,* they are caught up in its confusion and
fail to recognize the eternal *atman* in themselves.

When they recognize that they and the world soul are one, they are liberated, *moksha*. Then they are ready for reunion with *Brahman*. They experience *nirvana* and on physical death it will no longer be necessary for them to be reborn.

Nirvana is a fascinating word made up of two particles: *nir,* which is a negative, and *va,* which is the root of the verb "to blow." *Nirvana* then is the "blowing out" or the "going out" of the fires of life. It is the "fires" of life, the passions and emotions, which bind a person to the illusory world of *maya.* As the individual puts them out *(nirvana)* one by one, his consciousness of himself as eternal *atman* becomes more and more clear. In a beautiful simile, upon entrance into *nirvana,* the individual soul is absorbed into God as a single drop of water is defused in the sea. A person loses individuality forever, but he does not cease to exist. Thereafter he exists as part of the greater reality of God.

The immanent God

The heart of classical Hinduism is its pantheism, the fundamental assumption that all that exists is *Brahman.* The *Bhagavad Gita* expresses it sublimely:

> I am the self in the inmost heart of all that are born. . . .
> I am their beginning, their middle, and their end. . . .
> I am the beginning, the middle, the end, of all creation. . . .
>
> I am unending time,
> I am the ordainer who faces all ways,
> I am destroying death,
> I am the source of all that is to be. . . .
> I am the glory of the glorious,
> I am victory, I am courage,
> I am the goodness of the virtuous. . . .
> I am the force of those who govern,
> I am the statecraft of those who seek to conquer,

> I am the silence of what is secret,
> I am the knowledge of those who know,
> And I am the seed of all that is born. . . .
>
> There is nothing that can exist without me.
> There is no end to my holy powers. . . .
> And whatever is mighty or fortunate or strong
> Springs from a portion of my glory (10.20-41).[1]

However, as we noted earlier, human ignorance can mask God's reality and lead people to believe that the passing world of *maya* is real. This ignorance is addressed in Svetaketu's famous conversation with his father in the *Chandogya Upanishad* 6.12:

> "Bring me a fruit from this banyan tree."
> "Here it is, father."
> "Break it."
> "It is broken, Sir."
> "What do you see in it?"
> "Very small seeds, Sir."
> "Break one of them, my son."
> "It is broken, Sir."
> "What do you see in it?"
> "Nothing at all, Sir."
>
> Then his father spoke to him: "My son, from the very essence in the seed which you cannot see comes in truth this vast banyan tree. Believe me, my son, an invisible and subtle essence is the Spirit of the whole universe." [2]

The practical outcome of this belief is that the Hindu sees the divine in everything. As diverse as nature and life are, these differences are merely aspects of God, whose being is so incredibly rich that he is found in everything, and everything that exists is found in him. The different aspects of being are merely the "thousand faces" of God.

> O *Brahman* Supreme!
> Formless art thou, and yet
> (Though the reason none knows)
> Thou bringest forth many forms;
> Thou bringest them forth, and then
> Withdrawest them to thyself.
> Fill us with thoughts of thee!

Thou art the fire,
Thou art the sun,
Thou art the air,
Thou art the moon,
Thou art the starry firmament,
Thou art *Brahman* Supreme:
Thou art the waters . . . . thou
The creator of all!

Thou art woman, thou art man,
Thou art the youth, thou art the maiden,
Thou art the old man tottering with his staff;
Thou facest everywhere.

Thou art the dark butterfly,
Thou art the green parrot with red eyes,
Thou art the thunder cloud, the seasons, the seas.
Without beginning art thou,
Beyond time, beyond space,
Thou art he from whom sprang
The three worlds.

One thou art, one only.
Born from many wombs,
Thou hast become many:
Unto thee all return.
Thou, Lord God, bestowest all blessings,
Thou the Light, thou the Adorable One.
Whoever finds thee
Finds infinite peace
　　　(*Svetasvatara Upanishad* 4).[3]

In Hindu thinking, God is the life of nature in the same way as the spirits of women and men are their life. The universe surges with creative vigor. The divine is to be found everywhere, not only in a single God or a number of Gods, but in human beings, in animals, in trees, and even in rocks and rivers. Hindus rub shoulders with God in every field and in every street. They are on comparatively familiar terms with him, both in his friendly and in his awful manifestations.

The Hindu experiences God in nature: in the sea and in the good earth that is his home, in the beauties of the earth and the glory of the night sky.

God is present in every grain of sand, in every clod of earth, in every flower, and in every leaf. His power is manifest in the miracle of the seed, in the brightness and warmth of the sun, and in the clouds covering the sky that bring rain to the earth.

However, the Hindu need not look at the outer world to find evidence of the divine. God is present in the beauty and the tragedy of people's lives, in their daily work, and in their relationships with other persons. Nor is he to be found only among the lords of the earth, the rich and the powerful, the mighty who make decisions guiding the destinies of nations. The lowliest laborers, farmers, and fishermen are in no way devoid of the divine presence. God is to be found in all that has any merit, strength, or value. This aspect of Hinduism leads to a deep nature mysticism or pantheism.

Ahimsa

Since the universe is alive with God, people encounter him in all things. The Hindu has a very profound sense of this encounter and therefore will not violate this presence of God in either living or non-living things. The name for this teaching is *ahimsa*. The word means "non-injury" or "nonviolence" to living things. Albert Schweitzer, the great 20th-century Christian, coined the term "reverence for life" for this ideal. The Hindu sees God in other people and in the entire animal world. The goal of *ahimsa* is gentleness out of respect for the divine spirit that is in all that exists.

The people of India love animals and respect the divine gift of life in them, never taking animal life needlessly. Hindus are uncomfortable unless surrounded by the many animals of nature, and they make a place for them and provide for their needs.

They are accustomed to having animals in their home and near at hand.

Hindus also celebrate God's presence in inanimate nature. They not only surround themselves with animal life, but they strive to "tread lightly" on nature itself. The simple blessings of sunshine, water, and soil witness to them of God's bounty. Hindus try to use these resources without abusing them. To the best of their ability they try to use only what is absolutely necessary to survival and to waste as little as possible.

Ahimsa was originally the teaching of Mahavira, the founder of the Jains, a sect within Hinduism. The Jains who follow Mahavira sweep a path, or a chair, with a branch of leaves or a broom before stepping on the path or sitting on the chair. The more strict among them strain their drinking water and breathe through a piece of cloth to prevent injury to any living beings in the air or water.

Since God is in everything, Hindus practice nonviolence toward everything: rivers, mountains, trees, animals, insects, snakes, birds, etc. The Indian affection for the cow is an example of this attitude. The cow was originally a totem animal sacred to the Aryan invaders of India. To kill a cow is as serious a crime as murder. For a Hindu to eat beef is equivalent to cannibalism. Indians have become violently sick upon learning that they have inadvertently eaten beef in the West. Cows wander unmolested through the cities of India today, and it is the duty of a Hindu to protect them. Some will bow respectfully to cows as they pass, and wealthy men endow hostels for the care of old and decrepit cows.

Born in Kathiawar, where the Jains are strong, Mahatma Gandhi was deeply influenced by the ideal of *ahimsa*. Like many Hindus, he revered the cow as a great mother symbol, an example of gentleness,

and the nourisher of humanity. In trying to devise
a method the Indian minority might use to oppose
the discrimination shown toward them by the white
ruling classes in South Africa, Gandhi transformed
ahimsa (nonviolence) into *satyagraha* (truth-force).

The brute-force of the human animal nature contrasts with the truth-force of humanity at its spiritual best. The abused minority in South Africa had
the choice of violent revolution, which would almost
certainly have been put down with greater violence,
or some alternative method. From the ideal of
ahimsa, the Sermon on the Mount, and the writings
of the Christian pacifist Leo Tolstoy, Gandhi forged
satyagraha into a method of nonviolent resistance.

The route was bitterly difficult, but ultimately the
way of *satyagraha* was victorious in South Africa
and provided Gandhi with a practical tool for the
freeing of India from centuries of colonial rule.

The soul

At the deepest level the human self is identical
with the ground of the universe. Only *Brahman* and
the human soul are changeless in a world of time
and space undergoing incessant change. In one of
the earliest of the Upanishads, the *Chandogya,* the
sage Uddalaka says to his son Svetaketu: "That
which is the finest essence . . . this whole world has
that as its soul. That is reality. That is *atman.* That
art thou, Svetaketu." [4] In Sanskrit this famous
dictum reads: *tat tvam asi, that* you are, or you are
that. The heart of the pantheism of classical Hinduism is the recognition that the human self and the
world self are the same, and that they are alone
immortal in a universe of change.

> There is ONE . . . who governs the worlds
> with his power. . . . Greater than all is *Brahman,*

the Supreme, the Infinite. He dwells in the
mystery of all beings according to their forms
in nature. Those who know him who knows all,
and in whose glory all things are, attain immor-
tality. . . . His infinity is beyond what is great
or small, and greater than him there is nothing . . . .

He is the inmost soul of all, which like a little
flame the size of a thumb is hidden in the hearts
of men. . . . God is in truth the whole universe:
what was, what is, and what beyond shall ever
be. . . . He knows all, but no one knows him. . . .

Concealed in the heart of all beings lies the
atman, the spirit, the self; smaller than the
smallest atom, greater than the greatest spaces.
When by the grace of God man sees the glory
of God, he sees him beyond the world of desire
and then sorrows are left behind (*Svetasvatara
Upanishad* 3).[5]

In Hinduism all things *are* God.

He who, dwelling in the earth, yet is not earth,
whom the earth does not know, whose body the
earth is, who controls the earth from within . . .
He is your Atman, the ruler within, the immortal.

He who, dwelling in the waters, yet is not the
waters, whom the waters do not know, whose
body the waters are, who controls the waters
from within . . . He is your Atman, the ruler
within, the immortal.

He who, dwelling in the fire, yet is not the
fire, whom the fire does not know, whose body the
fire is, who controls the fire from within. . . . He
is your Atman, the ruler within, the immortal.

Thus atmosphere
     wind
     sky
     sun
     space
     moon and stars
     ether
     darkness
     light

     all things
     breath
     the tongue

the eye
the ear
the mind
the semen.
He is the unseen seer, the unheard hearer,
the unthought thinker, the unknown knower.
There is no hearer but he. There is no thinker
but he. There is no knower but he. He is your
Atman, the ruler within, the immortal (*Brihad-
Aranyaka Upanishad* 3.7).[6]

If the human self is a fragment of a far greater
world soul, then humanity is not alien in this universe, but part of the greater reality of this world.
Classical Hinduism spares the people of India such
anxiety and alienation. Rather than feeling isolated
from the world, or orphaned in an uncaring world,
Hindus believe themselves to be a part of a divine
reality filling the entire world. They are not cut off or
alienated from their world. They are, in every way
and in every thing they do, an integral part of its
life.

The spiritual and the material

A further inference from the conception of
the divine found in classical Hinduism is that
only spirit is real, *maya* is not. The world of time
and space, *maya,* is endlessly subject to change.
Within this changing world in which nothing lasts,
only the reality of the divine spirit is permanent,
changeless, and worthy of human reliance. Whoever
relies on the changing world of *maya* is bound
ultimately to be disappointed and disillusioned.

This material world of our senses, this *maya*
which we inhabit day by day, emerges from *Brahman,* the Hindu teachers say, like smoke arising from
a fire. The smoke is not the fire, yet it comes from
the fire and cannot exist without it. People are
tempted to regard the world of time and space,

maya, as the only real world. As a result they may spend their lives trying to build something permanent in this world.

This present world is not of lasting value or meaning. Although the great mass of people may live for *maya,* because they do not know better, here and there a few individuals will catch some glimpse of the eternal in the midst of time. Such uncommon persons will come to understand that, all appearances notwithstanding, all that really matters is spirit.

Many paths to the truth

In its bewildering diversity Hinduism makes room within itself for radically different religious understandings and life-styles. As a result, it is often described not as a religion, but as a family of religions. There are various types of Hinduism, which supplement but rarely exclude one another. What may appear at first to be confusing is actually a source of strength, however. Every Indian can find something meaningful out of the rich variety of Hindu paths.

In the *Bhagavad Gita,* the most sacred of Hindu scriptures, four *margas* (paths) or *yogas* (disciplines) are named as the major alternatives among which the Hindu can choose: *karma-yoga,* the way of action; *jnana-yoga,* the way of learning and insight; *bhakti-yoga,* the way of personal relationship with God; and *raja-yoga,* the way of self-development by means of rigorous discipline.

Karma-yoga

Karma-yoga, the way of action, is a very old way. In the *Vedas,* the earliest Hindu sacred writings, it is the way of ritual and sacrifice. However, an important transformation of the way of action takes place in the *Gita*. Here *karma-yoga* is defined as action outside the home for the welfare of others. Before that time the renunciation of life in the world was generally thought to be necessary for a person seeking liberation *(moksha)*. The *Gita* argues that such renunciation is not essential, and that liberation can be won through significant work in the world. The way of *karma-yoga* is for active people who choose to perform tasks in the spirit of egoless renunciation of the consequences of their labor.

> Set thy heart upon thy work, but never on its reward. Work not for a reward; but never cease to do thy work. Do thy work in the peace of yoga and, free from selfish desires; be not moved in success or in failure. Yoga is evenness of mind— a peace that is ever the same (2.47-48).[7]

Let people do what is right, and let what follows follow. Let people do their duty with a "holy indifference for the results." The results or consequences of the work must be devoted to God; then the work can be done unselfishly in a free and detached spirit.

> By doing the work that is proper to him and rejoicing in the doing, a man succeeds, perfects himself. . . . By dedicating the work . . . to him who is the source of the activity of all beings, by whom this whole universe was spun, a man attains perfection and success *(Bhagavad Gita* 18.45-46).[8]

People cannot live without acting, and all actions bind them to the world of *maya.* How are they ever to be freed from the normal consequences of their actions? The message of the *Gita* is, let them take virtuous action while remaining inwardly detached from what they are doing.

Let a person do God's will for himself, but accept
failure as gladly as he would welcome success. Let
him offer the consequences of his actions to God, to
whom they ultimately belong, and in this way be
oblivious to the rewards of his just action.[9]

The *Gita* reads:

> Do the work that is prescribed for you. . . .
> Therefore detached, perform unceasingly the
> works that must be done, for the man detached
> who labors on to the highest must win through.
> . . . As witless fools perform their works at-
> tached to the work they do, so, unattached,
> should the wise man do, longing to bring about
> the welfare of the world (3.3, 3.8, 3.19, 3.25).[10]

Mahatma Gandhi is India's greatest modern example of a *karma-yogi*. Before he led his people to in-
dependence from the British and in reforming Hindu
society, he renounced his own interests and concerns.
Gandhi believed that one must prepare for leadership of the nation by abandoning satisfaction of individual needs and pleasures. He believed voluntary
poverty and sexual chastity were required of him.
Another person might find other desires standing in
his way. Freed from selfish needs in this way, an individual can work unselfishly in a free and detached
way for the greater good of humanity.

Jnana-yoga

The second yoga is *jnana*, the yoga of knowledge
or insight. This is the path of classical Hinduism
that appeals to the philosophical, intellectual, and
contemplative person. Ignorance masks the truth
that the human self and the world self are the same
fundamental substance. Through study of the Upani-
shadic texts, and above all by reflection and contemplation, a person can come to the insight that

human nature and the divine nature are, at the root, one. Liberation *(moksha)* is the result.

To "become *Brahman*" means detachment from all outside interests and integration of the self. For the integrated person, all distinctions between the world within and the world without, between the knower and what is known, between subject and object, fade, because *Brahman* is everywhere the same.

> For upon this athlete of the spirit whose mind is stilled, the highest joy descends: all passion laid to rest, free from all stain, *Brahman* he becomes. . . . With self integrated by spiritual exercise now he sees the self in all beings standing, all beings in the self: the same in everything he sees *(Bhagavad Gita* 6.27, 6.29).[11]

Here integration means oneness of all beings with the self, and of the self with all that exists. People "become *Brahman*" and so know themselves to be a fragment of the eternal reality underlying the universe.

This insight cannot be learned the way students acquire knowledge in a classroom. People cannot be *told* they and ultimate reality are one. They must *experience* its truth; the truth must come as insight. When this insight *(jnana)* comes, they can pass beyond the sphere of action *(karma)* into the realm of wisdom and perfect peace.

Bhakti-yoga

However, neither *karma-* nor *jnana-yoga* was to provide the religious path taken by the millions of India's common people. The first seemed tailored to the needs of very high-caste Hindu or, at the very least, uncommon individuals like Gandhi who were ready to serve the welfare of others selflessly. The second appealed to an educated and intellectual elite with the leisure to pursue its ideals. The great mass of people fit neither of these descriptions. They longed for a path more commensurate with their needs. Although they were not high caste, uncommon leaders, or intellectuals, they could show loving personal devotion to God.

In fact, it is this personal relationship between God and the individual that most distinguishes *bhakti* from other Hindu paths. God is not viewed as impersonal *Brahman*, but as a personal being full of grace and love for all his creatures. So intense is believers' devotion that they recognize their absolute dependence on God, apart from whom they can do nothing. They abandon themselves to God, put themselves completely in his hands, trust in him, and wait confidently for his grace.

If *grace* is a descriptive Western term we must use with caution, *savior* is another often applied to the God of *bhakti* devotion. In the *Gita* we read:

> Give ear to this my highest word, of all the most mysterious: "I love you well." Therefore will I tell you your salvation. Bear Me in mind, love Me and worship Me, sacrifice, prostrate yourself to Me: so will you come to Me, I promise you truly, for you are dear to Me. . . . Turn to Me, your only refuge, for I will deliver you from all evils; have no care (18.65-66).[12]

In passages like these, traditional Hindu virtues of renunciation and self-forgetfulness are transformed. The Hindu God becomes the refuge who saves people from the threat of old age and death. The clear teaching of *bhakti* Hinduism is that no matter how low people's social status, they have direct access to God as savior. By devotion to the Lord, common people can be saved and dwell in union with God.

Raja-yoga

However, it is none of these three yoga disciplines which has caught the imagination of people in the West today. Instead it is *raja-yoga,* "royal" yoga, the background for all practice of meditation, which commands the Westerner's interest.

No one can trace the origins of *raja-yoga.* They lie somewhere in the primordial Indian past. However, in historical times they owe much to the *yoga sutras* of Patanjali, a famous teacher who lived in approximately the second century B.C. The term *yoga* means to bring together, to couple, to yoke. What is sought is union with the divine. By inference the word also means the religious discipline by which such union can be achieved. Various practices are used to withdraw consciousness from the periphery of life to its center, from the material world of the senses to the inner world of the spirit. Many scholars consider yoga to be the earliest system of self-transformation.

Yoga is a system of body disciplines designed to prepare for the much more difficult task of disciplining the spirit. Certainly the spirit cannot be trained until the body is first brought under control. The basic principle of the discipline is limitation of activities and distractions. Once the body has been stilled, the *yogi* can begin to discipline the spontaneous wandering of the mind.

The mind is restless. . . . It is hard to train. . . . But by constant practice and by freedom from passions the mind in truth can be trained.[13] The goal is to discipline the mind to ignore diversions so a deeper level of consciousness can be reached. Here is a classical description of the *yogi,* in the *Bhagavad Gita:*

> Let him set up for himself a steady seat in a clean place. . . . There let him sit and make his mind a single point, let him restrain the opera-

tions of his thought and senses. . . . Remaining
still, let him keep body, head, and neck in a
straight line, unmoving: let him fix his eye on
the tip of his nose, not looking round about
him. . . .

All contact with things outside he puts away,
fixing his gaze between the eyebrows; inward
and outward breaths he makes the same as they
pass up and down the nostrils. With senses,
mind, and soul restrained, the silent sage, on
deliverance intent, who has forever banished
fear, anger, and desire, is truly liberated.

There let him sit, his self all stilled, his fear
all gone, firm in his vow of chastity, his mind
controlled. . . . Then will he approach that peace
which has nirvana as its end (6.11-13; 5.27, 28;
6.14-15).[14]

Progress in *raja-yoga* proceeds through eight
stages, according to Patanjali's system:

1. *Yama,* or self-control. As the first step in the
program of growth, the *yogi* sets about practising
the five moral rules or precepts which originated
with the Jains: *ahimsa* (nonviolence), truthful-
ness, honesty, sexual chastity, and avoidance of ac-
quisitiveness.

The uniquely Indian ideal of *ahimsa* we have already discussed. The central ideals are among those
in the Mosaic Ten Commandments. However, the
fifth ideal, like the first, is strange to the values
widely held in the West. Not being possessive means
literally not wanting to own the products of the
earth and to have them as one's own. The feeling of
ownership, especially exclusive ownership, is to be
avoided. The reason is that this sense of ownership
leads to attachment to possessions and binds the person to the earth. As a result, many older Hindus,
after the child-bearing years are over, pursue a
course of radical dispossession. This is the essential

first step. There is no possibility of developing beyond this point until these five rules are kept.

2. *Niyama,* or observing the rules of self-discipline
in such a way as to create an environment in which
further spiritual growth is possible. Some of the
features of such an environment are solitariness,
serenity, study, and dedication to the ideal of cultivation and development of the self.

This step in *raja-yoga* expresses a profound truth
about human life. Every person needs a serene environment permitting profound thought, self-analysis, and the practice of a spiritual discipline.

3. *Asanas,* or disciplining the body so as to be able
to assume the proper postures. Under the name
hatha-yoga, these are the well-known physical exer-
cises and positions of the body that millions in the
West have found valuable.

The goal of *raja-yoga* is to free the person from
distractions and to permit development of the mind
and the experience of higher states of consciousness.
Distractions are of various kinds: those of the world
surrounding the *yogi,* those of the body, and those
of the mind. No one can be free of mental distractions while still distracted by the body. In order to
reach a bodily condition that will permit prolonged
mental alertness, without the bodily distractions, the
body must be disciplined.

The *asanas* are postures that are practiced so they
can be performed relatively effortlessly and held for
long periods of time. While there are thousands of
asanas, the most famous is *padmasana,* the lotus posture, in which a person assumes an upright sitting
position, with the spine in a straight line from head
through shoulders to back, sitting cross-legged with
the feet placed on the opposite thighs. This is the
classic posture of meditation.

4. *Pranayama,* or control of breathing. Of all the

body's functions, the one most apparent, continuously, is breathing. As a result, it can be a major distraction to the *yogi*, particularly if it is rapid or irregular. Thus breathing must be slow, deep, and rhythmical in meditation. This quiets an important bodily process. In this more relaxed state, the mind is freed from being disturbed by breathing.

5. *Pratyahara,* or withdrawal of the senses from all objects of perception. By no longer being sensitive to external stimuli, the *yogi* turns from the world outside to the world within: "When a man draws in on every side his senses from their proper objects as a tortoise its limbs, firm-stablished is the wisdom of such a man." [15]

Our senses are continually bombarded by thousands of sights, sounds, odors, flavors, and textures. The world is rich in diversity. Our senses have been trained to be responsive to these stimuli. *Pratyahara* is the discipline by which the senses are withdrawn, turned in upon the self, one by one. Each sense can be withdrawn: sight, hearing, smell, taste, touch, one at a time, until all are stilled.

6. *Dharana,* or concentration, steadying the mind. The mind is held steadily to the contemplation of a single object or idea until it is emptied of everything else. This is the first of the last three steps of *raja-yoga* which deal with direct discipline of the mind. As they are stages in a single process, it is difficult to draw sharp lines of demarcation between them. In *dharana* traditional objects upon which to concentrate the mind have been the navel, the tip of the nose, and the "third eye" midway between the eyebrows. A pebble may be used. The Buddha often used a flower.

The goal of *dharana* is to focus the mind on one object or idea so as to discipline the "restless" intellect, which is drawn continually to a diversity of objects and experiences. The goal of *dharana* is singleness of mind, effectively shutting out multiplicity. The object or idea or process used for concentration must not arouse interest in itself. It is to hold the mind transfixed, but possess no intrinsic interest.

7. *Dhyana,* or meditation. Meditation moves from singleness of mind to the integration of consciousness. The term *integration* has a twofold meaning. First, it means integration of the self, unity or wholeness. Yoga and meditation were widely viewed as therapeutic in ancient India, as they are by many young Westerners today.

Second, meditation is also integration of the *yogi* and the greater external reality. On both counts, integration of the self and integration with the world beyond the self, meditation is a healing experience.

8. *Samadhi,* or trance. It is impossible to draw a line between integration and trance. However, in trance the mind is emptied of all content. All activity of the intellect disappears, and only pure consciousness remains. First the mind becomes unconscious of any object *(dharana)*, then it becomes unconscious even of itself *(samadhi)*. The result is a superior consciousness in which neither subject nor object has any meaning.

In *samadhi,* the *yogi* experiences unity, identity, oneness. It is not so much that all differences seem merged or obliterated, but in this superior state of consciousness, the *yogi* perceives the fundamental sameness of everything that exists.

The goal of *samadhi* is to experience a state without sensation, without thought, and finally without consciousness itself. According to Hindu thought, this overcoming of opposites is not only a state of experience that can be reached by the human mind, but it is also the goal of self-realization. The most important Indian symbol for this goal is the zero. The zero or *bindu* means "dot," "seed," "semen." While the zero-point can mean nothingness or emptiness, it also means fullness or wholeness.

This paradoxical use of language expresses exactly the experience of *samadhi*. In the "emptiness" of *samadhi*, there is an experience of the wholeness in which all the opposites meet and are overcome: subject and object, past and future, male and female, high and low, darkness and light.

Thus emptiness is fullness. The highly disciplined emptiness of *samadhi* is the necessary prerequisite for the experience of wholeness. The *yogi* who has reduced himself to zero experiences all things.

The classic description of the *yogi* who has reached this point is found in the *Gita:*

> When thought, held well in check, is stilled in self alone, then is a man from longing freed though all desires assail him: then do men call him integrated. As a lamp might stand in a windless place, unflickering . . . this likeness has been heard of such men of integration who control their thought and practice integration of the self. When thought by spiritual exercise is checked and comes to rest, and when of oneself one sees the self in self and finds content therein, that is the utmost joy which transcends all things of sense and which soul alone can grasp. When he knows this and knowing it stands still, moving not an inch from the reality he sees, he wins a prize beyond all others. . . . Therein he firmly stands, unmoved by any suffering, however grievous it may be. This he should know is what is meant by spiritual exercise, the unlinking of the link with suffering and pain. This is the act of integration that must be brought about with firm resolve and mind all undismayed. . . . For upon this athlete of the spirit whose mind is stilled the highest joy descends: all passion laid to rest, free from all strain, Brahman he becomes. And thus all flaws transcending, the athlete of the spirit, constant in integrating self, with ease attains unbounded joy, Brahman's

> touch. With self integrated by spiritual exercise,
> he sees the self in all beings standing, all beings
> in the self: the same in everything he sees
> (6.18-29).[16]

This is the supreme goal, to see all beings in the self and the self in all beings. It is the highest state to which the practice of *raja-yoga* can take a person.

Sadhana

In classical Hinduism the goal is discovering one's destiny as a spiritual being. However, there is nothing inevitable about this discovery. Each person must find a way (a *marga* or a *sadhana*) for making the discovery, a pilgrimage along a particular path unique to his or her situation. The distant destination is spiritual realization, but it can only be reached by a route mapping each stage along the way. A *sadhana* is the charted process of spiritual growth aimed at bringing a person to a goal through a graduated series of steps.

In addition to accurate blueprints, an artisan needs proper tools. We often say that having the right tool is half the job. The same is true of spiritual growth. The spiritual quest requires discipline of mind and spirit. These tools equip people to make the fullest use of their spiritual capacities, shaping the rough wood of the inner self into a more pleasing form.

If one asks a Hindu what religion he follows, one commonly asks him what yoga he follows. Since *yoga* also means method or discipline, the force of the question is to ask him what discipline he has undertaken. Indian religion is not a set of beliefs, but a discipline to be followed. The lack of a gap between belief and practice is a traditional strength of the Hindu religion.

Chapter 4

Sources in
the Buddhist tradition

Steve and Mary McKensie, who abandoned middle-class American city life for a commune in rural New Mexico, stand in a long tradition. They would probably not have identified Buddhism as part of it. But withdrawing from society and its values to pursue one's self-development is a very old ideal, going back to the *sannyasin* of India. India is the country in which withdrawal from society as the price of spiritual development originated.

The *sannyasin* broke all earthly ties and became a homeless wanderer. This was already an ancient ideal when the Buddha took it up 25 centuries ago. In the retelling of his life story, it is called the "great renunciation." However, the Buddha tempered the ideal, because he believed extreme asceticism could well be self-defeating and might not lead to spiritual growth at all. For those who wished to make their break with society cleanly, he established the way of *Bhikkhu* (monk) and *Bhikkuni* (nun). However, for the great majority of his followers, he counseled restriction of needs and simplification of life, very like that which the McKensies sought.

The Buddha's life story

Facts about the Buddha's life are meager. There is no continuous biography in the earliest scriptures, and many legends about him are factually untrue or historically without basis. However, the central legend surrounding him may be more important than his historical life, and perhaps more true as well. The symbols accurately reflect the real life, hidden from us now by the shadows of history. The legend follows.

The founder of the noble religion of Buddhism bore the name Siddhartha Gautama. He was born about 563 B.C. in the town of Kapilavastu in southern Nepal, in the shadow of the Himalayas about 100 miles north of Benares. His father, Suddhodana, was ruler of the Sakya people.

On the occasion of his son's birth, the raja was informed by an astrologer that Siddhartha either would become one of the greatest of earthly rulers or would abandon his royal heritage. He would be moved to take the latter course if he experienced the pain of human life or met a *sannyasin* who had forsaken the world. In this case he would abandon society and found a great world religion. As a royal father who wished his son to rule in his place one day, Suddhodana did his best to protect Siddhartha from such experiences. The raja built a great palace, set it in the middle of a vast park, and confined his son to a make-believe royal world.

The boy grew up amid the pleasures of the royal court. For all the contact he had with the real world, he might have been a prisoner in a castle of marble and gold. His life was happy, if happiness means protection from the unpleasant realities of life. He tasted every fruit from the tree of life. In due time his father provided a beautiful wife, and the young pair shared much happiness in each other's company.

Then the first cloud crossed Siddhartha's horizon. As time passed, the young couple remained childless. The young prince, who had never been denied anything, took to brooding. What was the meaning of this deprivation? Must human happiness always be marked by flaws like this? What is the meaning of life? What is the place of suffering in human experience?

Siddhartha concluded that the answers must be found outside the walls of his earthly paradise, so he commanded his charioteer, Channa, to take him out into the surrounding countryside. First they came upon a beggar covered with the sores of a loathsome disease. Gautama turned aside in horror, but the charioteer whispered, "This, my prince, is the way of life." Before he could absorb the shock of this discovery, the prince met an aged man, bent and broken by the weight of his years. "This too is the way of life," Channa said. They drove on, only to come upon a naked corpse, swollen, discolored, rotting in the sun. "This," said Channa, "is the *end* of life."

Siddhartha was still trying to assimilate the knowledge that human life becomes diseased, must grow old, and eventually must end, when he encountered a new experience. The chariot came upon a *sannyasin*. His peaceful expression and manner in the face of such human miseries made a very strong impression on the young prince.

A shaken Siddhartha returned to the royal residence. He had been brought face to face with the sobering realities of disease, old age, and death, and the effect upon him was unsettling.

At this point he learned that his wife was pregnant and would give birth in a few months. The raja planned a great banquet to celebrate the birth. A son was born, and the grandfather rejoiced in another heir. But within Siddhartha's breast, the conflict between a life of family and community responsibility and the promising liberation of the life of the *sannyasin,* the homeless wanderer, was already waging.

Guests came from every quarter to rejoice in the birth. The celebration went on for days and climaxed with a great banquet. All the aristocracy of the region was there. After much feasting, the revelry became more and more drunken. By early morning the guests were all asleep, many lying where they had fallen. Siddhartha alone was awake and sober. As he surveyed the scene of debauchery, he was revolted by its apparent meaninglessness. He concluded that the quest for sensual delight did not contain the secret of happiness. His royal life of self-indulgence, with its material comforts and earthly security, did not contain within it the meaning of life. He would have to seek elsewhere.

Siddhartha stole quietly to the door of his bedchamber and looked for a last time upon his sleeping wife and infant son. Then he tiptoed quickly away and ordered Channa to saddle two of his swiftest horses. They rode all night. By dawn they had reached the banks of a great river, the boundary of his father's domain. Siddhartha prepared to leave his homeland. He cut off his long, flowing hair, one of his marks as a prince, then stripped himself of his princely robes and jewelry and gave them to his servant. He commanded Channa to return to his home and to tell his family his decision. Then, newly shorn of his elegance as a prince, he put on the traditional yellow robe of the mendicant. The robe was the same as that worn by a condemned prisoner who had forfeited all claims on society. The young man who could not find the meaning of life as a prince now sought it at the other extreme of the social order.

This great story has awakened the admiration of Asia, and is the subject of some of the continent's splendid art. Deep in the human heart lies the expectation that life could be rid of its uncertainties if only people had wealth enough. Wealth can cover human nakedness and bring security in the midst of an otherwise precarious existence. The universal human symbol for this is a home. The dream is to possess wealth enough to build a home in a beautiful setting, and then to put a wall around it to shut out whatever is dangerous and painful in life. It is a primordial dream, longing for a secure retreat from life's harsh realities.

However, as Suddhodana learned, it is not a dream that can be sustained. No walls can shut life out. Human suffering unfailingly finds its mark in every person's life. A debilitating injury, an incurable disease, a crushing disappointment, a spiritual or mental disturbance—the unwelcome guest intrudes upon every life. The problem is not how to evade it, but rather how to deal with it when it inevitably comes. This Siddhartha understood at the time of the great renunciation.

So Siddhartha became an ascetic. He would meet life's sterner realities head on. He lived in the open, fasted, and renounced the satisfactions of normal human needs. He became a living skeleton. His ascetic endurance won him the admiration of five disciples. For six years he tried every avenue of asceticism, but finally he concluded that all of his rigors had brought him no closer to the truth. The problem of human suffering remained unsolved. He concluded that the way to peace of mind did not lie through agony of body. In fact, spiritual development required an alert mind in a healthy body. He had become so weakened by his austerities that he could barely function. A milkmaid came by and offered him a bowl of curds, and Siddhartha ate.

Neither his princely life of affluence nor his ascetic life of renunciation held the answer to life's riddle. He turned aside at a grove in a place called Bodh-gaya and sat at the foot of what is now called a *bodhi* (enlightenment) tree. There he began a process of thought and meditation that eventually became the four noble truths of Buddhism. Siddhartha sat at the base of the tree, facing east, and determined not to arise until he attained enlightenment. For 49 days and nights he kept his vigil, resisting every temptation. On the 50th day he experienced *nirvana,* the state of perfect inner peace, and enlightenment came. Now he understood the cause of human suffering and saw into the meaning of human existence. Siddhartha Gautama became the Buddha, the enlightened one.

Quite naturally he wanted to share his discovery, but he hesitated. Would people listen and understand? He concluded some, at least, would listen. Lest these perish without the understanding to which he had come, he chose to return to society out of compassion for them.

The Buddha set out for Benares to seek the five disciples who had forsaken him when he left the ascetic life. In the famous deer park just outside town, he found them and preached the first Buddhist sermon.

> There are two extremes, O Alsmen, which he who has given up the world ought to avoid. What are those two extremes? A life given to pleasures, devoted to pleasures and lusts; this is degrading, sensual, vulgar, ignoble, and profitless. And a life given to mortifications; this is painful, ignoble, and profitless. By avoiding these two extremes the Truthfinder (Tathagata) has

gained the knowledge of the Middle Path which
leads to insight, which leads to wisdom, which
conduces to calm, to knowledge, to enlightenment, to Nirvana. [1]

Here in short is the Buddhist "middle way," the
way between the extremes of the Buddha's self-indulgence in the affluent life of a prince and the self-
renunciation of his life as a religious ascetic.

The Buddha's preaching was so persuasive that
many became advocates of his teaching. True to his
decision to preach his insights abroad, the Buddha
sent his followers out into the world with this
famous exhortation:

> Go ye forth, brethren, on your journey, for the
> profit of the many, for the bliss of the many,
> out of compassion for the world, for the welfare,
> the profit, the bliss of devas and mankind!
> Go not any two together. Proclaim, brethren,
> the Dharma, goodly in its beginning, goodly in its
> middle, goodly in its ending. Both in the spirit
> and in the letter do ye make known the all-per-
> fect, utterly pure righteous life. There are be-
> ings with but little dust of passion on their eyes.
> They are perishing through not hearing the
> Dharma. There will be some who will under-
> stand.[2]

Buddhism became the first great missionary religion in history, predating Christianity's missionary thrust by five centuries and Islam's by eleven.
For 45 years the Buddha moved from place to place
in northeast India, preaching to all who came to him.

After so long a time, in the fullness of his years,
the Buddha knew himself to be dying. He addressed
the sermon of the great passing to his followers.
Among his words were these:

> "Be islands unto yourselves, Ananda! Be a
> refuge to yourselves; do not take to yourselves
> any other refuge. See truth as an island, see
> truth as a refuge. Do not seek refuge in anyone

but yourselves. . . . And whoever, Ananda, now or after I am dead, shall be an island unto themselves and a refuge to themselves, shall take to themselves no other refuge, but seeing truth as an island, seeing as a refuge truth, shall not seek refuge in anyone but themselves . . . it is they, Ananda, among my disciples, who shall reach the further shore! But they must make the effort themselves. . . .

"It may be, Ananda, some of you will have the idea 'The word of the teacher is no more, and now we are without a leader!' But, Ananda, you must not think of it like this. The Dharma, and the rules of the Sangha which I have expounded and laid down for you, let them, after I am gone, be your teacher."

Then the Buddha addressed the monks and said: "This I tell you, Bhikkhus, Decay is inherent in all conditioned things. Work out your own salvation with diligence." [3]

Radical simplification of life: The four noble truths

The heart of the Buddha's teaching is contained in the four noble truths. The first three of these are a kind of syllogism tracing the steps in his thinking as he grappled with the riddle of human life. They represent the substance of his enlightenment and contain his analysis of the human predicament and his answer to the problems it poses.

The first of the four noble truths defines the problem of human life as seen by the Indian culture into which the Buddha was born. It provides clues to the "solution" the other noble truths contain. The first noble truth is that all forms of life are subject to *dukkha*. The word is usually translated "suffering," but its true meaning is closer to "impermanence." Impermanence and change are the stuff of life. Nothing is precisely the same as it was a moment ago. Human institutions—universities, corporations, governments—built to last forever, grow old, decay, and die. Empires and dynasties do the same. Even those great monuments to the human spirit, the pyramids of ancient Egypt and the cathedrals of medieval Europe, slowly crumble and turn to dust.

Our relationships with loved ones are also impermanent, causing suffering. This point is made in the Buddhist scriptures in the famous story of Kisagotami, a young mother. Kisagotami's baby was bitten by a snake. Fearing that he might die, she came to the Buddha and asked him for something to cure her son. The Buddha sent her to find a measure of black mustard seed, stipulating that it had to come from a household where neither father, mother, child, nor slave had died.

Kisagotami went searching at once. Everywhere she went people were gracious and offered her the mustard when she told her story. But when she asked whether anyone in that household had died, she learned that the family had lost a member, and sadly gave the mustard back. At last she returned to the Buddha to tell him that she could not find the medicine he had sent her to discover. But he answered her, "Kisagotami, you have found the answer. Your baby was already dead when you brought him to me. Today you learned the universality of death. Not one family you visited has managed to escape it. Your loss is all mankind's loss. Bury your child!"

So the first of the four noble truths contains Buddhism's diagnosis of the predicament of human life. Life and all of its relationships and all of its achievements are subject to change, impermanence, and decay. It is this fact that Kisagotami and all mankind must come to understand.

The second of the four noble truths seeks to analyze the cause of this suffering *(samudaya)*. The cause of *dukkha* is *tanha*. The usual translation of *tanha* is "desire," or "thirst," or "craving." It means the fundamental drive for self-preservation and self-aggrandizement, the desire to preserve one's life and to have more for oneself. This desire binds a person to life, and leads to attachment, to involvement, and to a "clinging to existence."

The person who clings to life becomes bound in on every side by the affairs of the world. The desire to protect and preserve one's life means many attachments and much involvement. Desires are needs requiring fulfillment, and filling them brings suffering.

Desire creates expectations. The desire for life kindles hope that life may be preserved. This hope is bound by the very nature of life to end in disillusionment, despair, and death. Therefore the belief that human desires and needs can be met is the most serious and fundamental of human illusions. Desire creates expectations and hopes for life that cannot possibly be fulfilled. The result is suffering.

The third of the four noble truths describes how universal suffering may be eliminated *(nirodha)*. The individual must uproot the cause of suffering, which is desire. If people can learn not to cling to anything in the world, they can be free. They must learn to cease to desire. They must learn to temper their expectations. If human longings are what ensnare people, so that suffering is inescapable, then they must learn to stop longing.

There are good longings and bad longings, and Buddhists distinguish between them, but *all* longings lead to attachment to life and therefore to suffering. The opposite of attachment is detachment. Buddhists may own possessions and have loved ones, but they must move through life with detachment and a certain disinterest toward both things and people.

To uproot desire and longing is perfect peace. This state of being, when perfectly attained, is *nirvana*. Those who realize *nirvana* are free from all worries and troubles. They do not regret the past, nor do they brood about the future. They live fully in the present, free from anxiety, serene and peaceful. This is the Buddhist goal.

The fourth of the four noble truths is the Buddhist way of life known as the noble eightfold path. We will study certain features of it in a moment. First, inferences must be drawn concerning the Buddhist analysis of the human predicament. The first thing the Buddha did in his search for the meaning of life was to shed all the excess baggage of his affluent life. Like Jesus, he realized how possessions bind one to life. He decided he could be rid of many things and manage perfectly well with a few things. A person who possesses little is not bound by his possessions. Having radically simplified life in this way, a person discovers how few things are really necessary.

The basic Buddhist principle is that many needs complicate, while few needs simplify. Animal life is uncomplicated in this sense, but the story of human civilization is the story of the increasing complication of needs. The "higher" the standard of living, apparently the more complicated the needs. If the Buddha's principle is correct, Westerners are more enslaved by things than people in less developed societies.

Material goods cannot give meaning to life or bring real happiness. All the great world religions teach that material goods do not create a shortcut to happiness. The meaning of human life is spiritual. Things cannot bring happiness, because things are the most transitory of possessions. They are not lasting and therefore cannot bring lasting happiness.

The story is told of advice the Buddha gave to his followers. He said they must learn to stop eating before they'd had enough to satisfy them or before they had had as much as they thought they needed. Then they must apply this principle to the whole of life. They must learn to simplify their lives. They must learn to have fewer needs. This is the only way to freedom from the thralldom to material things.

The noble eightfold path

The noble eightfold path is the logical extension of the understanding of human life contained in the first three noble truths. It is in fact the fourth truth. It is a way of life leading to decline in those desires that produce suffering and to growth in those qualities that ultimately bring liberation from life's entanglements.

The eight steps are divided among three major goals: wisdom, right conduct, and discipline of mind.

Wisdom

1. *Right understanding*   acceptance of the analysis of human life and the solution to the human predicament contained in the diagnosis of the Buddha.

2. *Right attitude*   a strong intention and motivation for self-development.

Conduct

3. *Right speech*   avoidance of damaging and hurtful speech prompted by ill will.

4. *right action*   defined in the five precepts:
> *ahimsa,* nonviolence toward living things, reverence for life
> honesty with respect to possessions
> sexual chastity
> truthfulness
> abstinence from the use of alcohol and drugs

5. *Right profession*   avoiding five kinds of work that bring harm to others: commerce in deadly weapons, in slaves, in meat (as a butcher), in alcoholic beverages, and in poisons.

Discipline of mind

6. *Right effort*   reliance on one's own effort where spiritual growth is involved.

7. *Right concentration*   limiting natural mental diffuseness by focusing on a single thought or object.

8. *Right meditation*   the experience of trance in which all feelings disappear and only tranquility remains.

The first two steps in the noble eightfold path involve acceptance of Buddhist theory. Accepting the diagnosis is followed by recognizing the Buddha's prescription. Only then can Buddhists commit themselves to the task of self-development through which the noble eightfold path is intended to take them.

Buddhist practice then follows upon the theory. Buddhists accept the ancient Indian ideal of *ahimsa*. They are gentle, nonviolent, and compassionate. They generally seek to live in harmony with nature. In seeking such harmony they wish to disturb plant and animal life as little as possible. Faithful Buddhists also interpret *ahimsa* to mean a vegetarian diet. They do not want to satisfy their personal needs at the cost of taking animal life. They feel a sense of kinship with the living world around them. Reverence for plants and animals also requires that the environment not be willfully and needlessly defaced and destroyed in the name of progress.

The follower of the Buddha must also refrain from the use of alcohol and drugs, because there are no chemical answers to life's problems. Solving life's riddle can only be an individual and inward thing.

Nothing that comes from without can be expected to supply an answer.

Alcohol and drugs are seen to be chemical substitutes for the inner calm and peace Buddhism is able to provide to those who take its method seriously. Buddhism teaches an inner and spiritual method of release in the place of an external and chemical one.

There is another reason Buddhists do not use drugs and alcohol. Because the enlightenment all Buddhists seek happens in the human mind and spirit, the mind and spirit are instruments that must remain unclouded. People cannot experience that inner calm and peace, which is the goal of the Buddhist method, unless their minds and spirits are free from all that would incapacitate them in their quest for enlightenment.

The third division in the noble eightfold path is *bhavana,* cultivation of the mind. When Buddhism began in the sixth century B.C., it shared in this common Indian ideal and adopted the *yogic* practices of posture, breathing, and control of the senses and thoughts. The *yogi* abandoned this unhappy world for a spiritual world beyond, turning away from the outer world of history to discover meaning in the world of inner consciousness. But Buddhist practice carried this course a step further. A person moved from concentration on some visual object or image to ponder the impermanence of earthly things, the frailty of human existence, and the insubstantiality of the human self.

From the Buddha his followers learned aversion for the passing earth. They were counseled to ponder the perishableness of the physical world, the fading of youthful strength and beauty, and the changes decay and death bring to all living things. Aversion for this passing world leads to turning inward to the world of the permanent and the eternal.

Such meditation brings insight, literally "sight within," discernment of the inner nature of things. The Buddhist sees with another vision, viewing the world from an entirely different perspective that belongs to another world. It is as if a person's previous sight had been a dream, in a common Indian analogy, and now the person has awakened to a vision beyond all common sense perception.

The Buddhist who has reached the end of the eight-fold path is "awakened," having conquered sensuality, ignorance, and the craving for the earth and the things of the earth. It is as if he has climbed the high Himalayas and now looks down with "higher vision" upon the steamy plains below.

Buddhist tolerance

Many philosophies and ideologies require submission to their unqualified authority. Buddhism makes no such demands. Buddhists believe the *dharma* (teaching) to be true, but they are convinced that all persons must prove that truth for themselves. It is in fact certain that truth can come to an individual in no other way.

Buddhist tolerance rests first of all on freedom of thought and experience. This freedom is absolutely necessary, the Buddha taught, because a person's spiritual "enlightenment" and growth are dependent on the individual's own grasp of the truth in personal experience. All persons must be free to hear the truth for themselves and to test and prove it in their own experience.

This is the least authoritarian of positions. The authoritarian mind will present only its own position and will despise and condemn the positions of others. On the question of authority the Buddha gave the following famous advice:

> Do not be led by reports, or tradition, or hear-say. Do not be led by the authority of religious texts, nor by . . . logic or inference . . . nor by . . . speculative opinions, . . . nor by the idea: "this is our teacher." But when you know for yourselves that certain things are unwholesome, and wrong, and bad, then give them up. . . . And when you know for yourselves that certain things are wholesome and good, then accept them and follow them *(Anguttara-Nikaya)*.[4]

In this remarkably comprehensive statement, the Buddha counsels his followers not to accept the authority of teachers, traditions, inspired scriptures, logic, or speculation.

Western religions have more commonly insisted that people accept their truth, without question, as the only truth. They speak of scriptures handed down by an unbroken tradition. Such an unbroken tradition the Buddha likened to a line of blind men, each accepting what the preceding generation had taught. Each generation accepted as authoritative what it had not proved for itself. Blind men indeed!

Buddhist tolerance rests secondly on the Buddha's unwillingness to force ideas on an unwilling hearer. Buddhism has been a great missionary religion from the start, when the Buddha decided to share the content of his "enlightenment" with others rather than merely experience its benefits for himself. The Buddha offered to all people the way to enlightenment that he had found to be true in his own experience, but he would not make converts in the usual sense of the word. The initiative to accept and adapt it to themselves had to lie within the hearers.

This remarkable tolerance has guided the spread of Buddhism throughout the Asian world. The greatest Buddhist ruler of India, the Emperor Asoka,

though an absolute monarch, refused to impose
Buddhism on the people of his vast empire. In one of
his famous rock edicts he left us his point of view:

> One should not honor only one's own religion
> and condemn the religions of others, but one
> should honor others' religions. . . . Whoever
> honors his own religion and condemns other re-
> ligions, does so indeed through devotion to his
> own religion, . . . but on the contrary, in so
> doing he injures his own religion more gravely.
> . . . Let all listen and be willing to listen to the
> doctrines professed by others.[5]

This spirit of tolerance is one of the most cherished
ideals of Buddhist conviction. It is a source of pride
for Buddhists that their faith spread throughout
the vast continent of Asia without persecution or the
shedding of blood.

Thirdly, Buddhist tolerance rests on the Buddha's
reluctance to associate truth with any specific position. Truth is greater than the labels we ascribe to it.
The truth is, after all, not Buddhist alone, nor Christian nor Muslim. No religious position, however profound, has a monopoly on truth. Truth is so ma-
jestic and many-sided that no one has the whole
truth. Those who understand this fully do not make
monopolistic claims for their positions. They respect
formulations of the truth different from their own,
and possess a broad tolerance toward the values
and thinking of others.

This discussion of Buddhist tolerance is best
closed with the Buddha's famous simile of his teaching as a raft for crossing a great river.

> "O bhikkhus, a man is on a journey. He comes
> to a vast stretch of water. On this side the shore
> is dangerous but on the other it is safe and
> without danger. No boat goes to the other shore
> which is safe and without danger, nor is there
> any bridge for crossing over. He says to himself:
> 'This sea of water is vast, and the shore on this

side is full of danger; but on the other shore it is safe and without danger. No boat goes to the other side, nor is there a bridge for crossing over. It would be good therefore if I would gather grass, wood, branches, and leaves to make a raft, and with the help of the raft cross over safely to the other side, exerting myself with my hands and feet.' Then that man, O bhikkhus, gathers grass, wood, branches, and leaves and makes a raft, and with the help of that raft crosses over safely to the other side, exerting himself with his hands and feet. Having crossed over and got to the other side, he thinks: 'This raft was of great help to me. With its aid I have crossed safely over to this side, exerting myself with my hands and feet. It would be good if I carry this raft on my head or on my back wherever I go.'

"What do you think, O bhikkhus? If he acted in this way would that man be acting properly with regard to the raft?" "No, Sir." "In which way then would he be acting properly with regard to the raft? Having crossed and gone over to the other side, suppose that man should think: 'This raft was a great help to me. With its aid I have crossed safely over to this side, exerting myself with my hands and feet. It would be good if I beached this raft on the shore, or moored it and left it afloat, and then went on my way wherever it may be.' Acting in this way would that man act properly with regard to that raft.

"In the same manner, O bhikkhus, I have taught a doctrine similar to a raft. . . . It is for crossing over, and not for carrying" *(Majjhima-Nikaya)*.[6]

The doctrine is a means only, a means for discovering the deepest purpose of human existence and for conveying the disciple through life on a course of self-development. It is not an end in itself. If some other variation of the doctrine, or another doctrine altogether, is able to bring the disciple to self-knowledge, then let it. Whatever vehicle will bear the disciple safely across the river is sufficient.

Chapter 5

Sources in the tradition of Zen

The 36 American men and women practicing *zazen* in the *zendo* in the mountains of California represent one of the earliest and most influential Oriental traditions to reach our shores, that of Zen Buddhism. Their "sitting quietly, doing nothing," their experience of mindfulness, set in a garden that is in every detail the embodiment of Japanese aesthetics, leaves the observer with unforgettable images. Mindfulness is a state of "awakening" or of becoming more fully conscious. The discipline of *zazen* is needed to break down habitual actions, thoughts, and emotions and to create the climate for becoming aware of the world as it really is. What is sought, at the most profound level, is an altogether different way of perceiving everything that exists.

The history of Zen is embodied in its name. Zen is the Japanese equivalent of the Chinese *Chan*, which is the equivalent of the Sanskrit *dhyana*, meaning "meditation." So Zen is "meditation" Buddhism. While literally correct, this definition hides as much as it reveals. Anyone who thinks of Zen as passive withdrawal into some quiet monastery misses the point.

Zen is Buddhism influenced by Chinese culture.

The history of Zen, then, is the passage of Buddhism from its native India to Nepal and Tibet, then across the high Himalayas to China, and, after centuries of modification, to Japan.

Gautama Buddha (563-483 B.C.), Lao-tsu (640-531 B.C.), and Kung Fu-Tzu (551-479 B.C.), the traditional founders of the three great religions of China, are roughly contemporaneous in the sixth and fifth centuries B.C. While the religion of the Buddha came from outside China, Taoism and Confucianism are indigenous faiths.

The Indian and Chinese spirits are very different. In contact with Taoism and Confucianism, Buddhism was modified by the Chinese. The ancient and brilliant culture of China was informed by its two native, ancestral faiths. They have often been described as representing two sides of the Chinese character. Taoism rests on an ancient nature worship, which taught that the cosmic order was natural and good. The heavenly movement of planets, stars, sun, and moon, and the orderly procession of the seasons were felt to set the true pattern for human life. Confucianism rests on an ancient reverence for ancestors, which was believed to strengthen the continuity and harmony between the living, the dead, and yet unborn generations of people. This regard for human values produced a broad humanism that has deeply influenced the Chinese character.

However, Taoism contributed most to molding Zen in the Chinese manner. Taoism rests on a nature mysticism not unlike that of many other ancient peoples. However, this mysticism was carried to logical conclusions that most other peoples were unwilling to draw. It was the orderliness *(li)* of nature that impressed itself on the Chinese spirit. Humanity's inner nature was seen as an extension of the nature of the universe. To follow one is to be in harmony with the other. The nature inside and outside of humanity meet and coalesce. This view of nature is most characteristic of the Chinese people.

The central term is *Tao,* which means "the way," the way things are, the orderly way of the natural world. The *Tao* is the powerful and mysterious force that causes the sun to rise and set, the rains to come in their season, crops and animals to thrive and flourish, and all of the other forces of the natural world to operate. The *Tao* cannot be defined, but it is nevertheless the ultimate source of all things. Nature's deepest mystery, the mystery of the creation, is the mystery of the *Tao.*

To come into harmony with nature, the individual must follow the natural way of the *Tao.* Such harmoniousness comes about by *wu-wei,* the Chinese term that literally means "not-doing." However, it does not mean avoiding action altogether, but rather avoiding all action that prevents things from taking their natural course. Put affirmatively, it means doing only what is natural and spontaneous. Only catastrophy follows from the attempt to oppose the *Tao.* Interfere with a thing's existence and it resists. The more strongly you interfere, the greater the resistance. Better to pursue the "actionless activity" of *wu-wei.*

To be in harmony with nature outside the self requires individuals to recover their own original nature. For this conception, Taoism employs symbols such as the uncarved block, raw silk, and the newborn child.[1] All symbolize the human person as natural and good before society sets about forcing the individual into some mold of its making. Before civilization arose, people lived in nature, simply, with few needs, content, taking pleasure in rustic tasks. But civilization brought striving for money, power, and influence. Ambition stirred and inevitably led to competition, which in turn led to aggression, which in turn led to violence. In this way the greatest of social evils arose. Not being content with what one has—wanting more, wanting what others have—is the source of all human misery.

The uncarved block, the individual's original nature, was free from such hostility and aggressiveness, so the goal of human life must be to shed all selfishness and ambition and recover one's innate self. The Taoist faith sets out to undo the damage done by society and to restore the individual's original spontaneity, *tzu-jan* in Chinese. Such spontaneity is natural and unselfconscious. It is a state of simple integrity in which the self acts freely and easily without societal discipline regulating it. When the self acts spontaneously and naturally, it begins to exercise the creative power of *te*. *Te* is the creativity flowing through the person who is liberated from formal and disciplined methods and techniques. In this sense, Taoism frees individuals from convention so they may exercise their creativity.

In naturalness, simplicity, spontaneity, the person returns to nature, both in the sense of a return to the individual's nature as it originally was, and also in a return by society to a more natural state. In this way one follows the Tao, learns its way, and seeks to conform to it. One ceases trying to remake nature and society according to some human plan.

Beyond the intellect

In these Taoist themes of naturalness, simplicity, and spontaneity, we can begin to sense the shape of Zen Buddhism. Zen is a new way of perceiving reality. Through Zen people desire to pass beyond the intellect, in a baffling yet fascinating way. The intellect is a marvelously developed, highly skilled in-

strument for sifting and acquiring knowledge. It becomes a knowledge machine, reducing things to
words and definitions and formulas. As a machine
it easily becomes the victim of its own efficiency
when reality is reduced to words, definitions, and
formulas. The mind becomes a cage, permitting the
individual to see and understand only data that its
method illuminates and shutting out what it does
not.

There are two kinds of knowing: primary and
secondary. All knowledge of the intellect is secondary
knowing. It is *knowledge about* something. It is the
knowledge of books and classrooms. In fact, its perfect example is a book. There is nothing so dead as
a book. At best it represents the author's primary
experience reduced to words on pages. The words
and pages are not the experience, not the knowledge.
They are merely an intellectual reflection of it.
Through the book people can be introduced to the
writer's experience, but they cannot really share in
it. No individual can ever *know* another's experience,
nor can it be written down.

Yet most knowledge is of this kind, learned rather
than experienced. It is the product of long years of
schooling. The vast learning of the past is trans-
mitted to us through words and books. It is not
necessary for us to reinvent the wheel every time we
make a new beginning. However, we pay a price for
other people's knowledge, secondhand knowledge.
We may *use* it, but it is not our own until we test it
in our own experience.

Primary knowing is to know directly, to perceive
immediately, to become aware, to experience for
oneself. No secondary proof is necessary, because the
knowledge has already been authenticated in the
individual's firsthand experience. This is very like
what the Chinese say about the *Tao*. It cannot be de-

fined; it must be discerned. The *Tao* is the action of
the universe following its natural way. To understand it, one must learn to perceive nature in a new
way. The *Tao* can be observed in the course things
take when they are permitted to proceed in their
natural way: the flight of a bird, the flow of a river,
the rising of the sun, the changes of the seasons.

For the Zen Buddhist, all secondary knowing
yields *conventional* knowledge, the knowledge of
words and symbols. Zen seeks to liberate individuals
from all conventional patterns of thought and conduct, so they may understand life as it really is.
Words measure, classify, and set bounds of meaning. They are the definitions and forms the mind
uses to comprehend the real world. By means of
words our minds designate abstract and conceptual
categories. Words, definitions, and "measures" may
be confused with the world being described and
measured. What if reality simply cannot be grasped
or measured by terms and words, which are products
of the human mind? This is exactly what the Zen
Buddhist is saying. The actual world cannot be
grasped in intellectual categories. The real world
is always more and greater than human words and
concepts can capture.

All words and concepts, then, all schools of
opinion, all systems of thought may serve as means
to the end of knowing, but they may also obscure
more than they illumine. Zen Buddhists are not
wholly against words. The danger is that words so
easily detach themselves from realities and turn
into abstract conceptions. Zen Buddhists oppose
empty abstractions. They want to experience and
handle the thing itself. They are practical. They
desire action, not speech. Zen Buddhists wish to
open the closed doors and windows of the mind, let-

ting light flood in so they can view reality in a wholly new and different way.

To achieve this goal, Zen points us to the realm of nonverbal experience, to what we see or feel rather than what we think or say. Zen Buddhists wish to experience the world directly, as it really is, unobscured by human symbols and definitions of thought. Zen directs people to the tangible, concrete, and actual, rather than to the abstract and conceptual. Zen Buddhists are deeply mystical and thus unerringly drawn to primary experience of the real world, which no human words or symbols can fully convey.

The disciplined way

We noted earlier that the term *Zen* is the Japanese equivalent for *dhyana* or meditation. However, it is a tradition of meditation very different from that found in India. In fact, it would not be inaccurate to say that Zen is distinguished from other forms of Buddhism, not by any teachings unique to it, but rather by the techniques it uses.

Bodhidharma, an Indian *Bhikkhu* who is the traditional founder of Zen in China, described his teaching in these four lines:

> A special transmission outside the scriptures
> No dependence upon words and letters
> Direct pointing to the soul of man
> Seeing into one's own nature.[2]

There are important clues here for understanding Zen's special genius. The techniques of Zen Buddhism are intended to bring the individual to direct knowing in the most effective ways possible. This important crossing from the river bank of second-hand knowing to the further shore of direct experience may be made by any raft or bridge. The vehicle is not an end in itself. Whatever will bear the individual safely to the other shore will do. The materials of the raft or bridge may be scriptures, statues of the Buddha, rituals, incense, chanting, beautiful robes, vows, etc.

Though Zen Buddhists use these familiar religious tools to achieve their ends, they have a curious scorn for such "helps." They are the ABCs, useful to some, but to be outgrown as soon as reasonably possible. They are religious toys[3] to be discarded in growing up. In a famous Zen analogy, they are like a finger pointing at the moon. It would be foolish to confuse the finger with the moon. Zen seeks to liberate its disciples from the usual religious devices.

Taoism and Zen Buddhism represent one side of the Chinese character and Confucianism the other side. Taoism and Zen afforded a way of liberation from social convention for those suffering the pressures of a very conformist Confucian society laying heavy stress on etiquette and propriety.

Zazen

In place of the usual techniques of religion, Zen developed methods of its own, the most important of which are *zazen*, the *mondo*, and the *koan*. We began this study with a brief description of a *zendo*, the meditation hall of a California Zen community. The hall is a long room with wide platforms (*tan*) down either side, where disciples meditate. The platforms are covered with *tatami*, woven mats of straw, and the disciples sit in two long rows facing each other.

The disciples sit in the yogic posture of *padmasana*, the famous lotus posture with legs crossed and feet upon the thighs. Their hands rest in their laps, with palms upward and thumbs touching. The back is straight and the eyes are open, directed to the floor in front of the disciple. Breathing is slow and rhythmic, from the abdomen.

The goal of these techniques is to master the mind. To achieve this more important end, the body must first be relaxed and the mind's natural inclination to divergence controlled. The purpose of *zazen* is to free the mind from having to think about the body and to control its distractions so that it may give its entire attention and energies to a single task. In the *zendo* this task is usually wrestling with a *mondo* or a *koan*, as we shall see.

The techniques of *zazen* were almost certainly adapted from the yoga of India. Many of the features are common. However, the aims of yoga and *zazen* are different. In classical yoga, the final goals are concentration, single-mindedness, and finally trance *(samadhi)*. In *zazen*, trance is not the desired outcome. The purpose is to prepare the mind for intensive concentration on a *mondo* or a *koan*.

From time to time the *zazen* is interrupted and the disciples walk briskly around the floor to refresh themselves. They also interrupt *zazen* for work in the Zen community, for meals, and for sleep. The daily schedule is very rigorous, with every moment of the waking day prescribed, because great intensity of concentration is needed to break through from secondhand knowledge to primary experience.

It seems strange to Westerners, with their busy lives, that devotees of Zen Buddhism would sit still for so many hours in *zazen*. It appears to them to be unproductive, a waste of time and talent. A zenrin poem has it:

> sitting quietly, doing nothing,
> spring comes, and the grass grows by itself.[4]

The disciple of Zen knows that action without understanding is futile. People who cannot sit quietly and observe the world as it really is do not really know the world.

The purpose of *zazen* is to quiet the mind and to experience reality directly. To do this, one must look at the world with a mind that is not thinking, i.e., using symbols, categories, and abstractions. On the other hand, *zazen* is not merely sitting with a mind blank to all the impressions of the senses. Nor is it concentration or "one-pointedness" of the mind in the yogic sense. It is an awareness, beyond thought, of the real world in all its concreteness. It is sensitivity to otherwise unheard sounds, unseen sights, unfelt impressions. It is a whole new perception of reality.

Mondo and koan

Zen Buddhism has much in common with other forms of religion, but its methods are altogether unique. The experience of enlightenment sought is *satori,* and the methods are the *mondo* and the *koan*. It is difficult to distinguish the latter, because they are intimately interrelated. The *mondo* is a question-and-answer dialog between a master and pupil. The *koan* is a problem posed to the pupil by the master, based on actions and sayings of great Zen masters from the past. There is no rational solution to the problem. The question and answer appear unrelated, and the whole exchange baffles the intellect. The purpose of both *mondo* and *koan* is to force the pupil to recognize that there is no intellectual solution. They serve as preparation for transcending the intellect altogether.

Hence Zen literature is not discursive, because logical thinking, abstract statement, and conceptual reasoning lead to grave misunderstandings of the true meaning of Zen experience. The literature of Zen is little more than collections of anecdotes, incidents, dialog—i.e., *mondos* and *koans*.

The relationship between master and pupil is uniquely Asian. Classically, this relationship is one of greatest intimacy, for the master's role is to *initiate* the disciple into hidden mysteries. The student owes the teacher implicit obedience and respect, as great as for his own father, because the *guru* has become his spiritual father.

In the Orient, the master is called *roshi* and possesses great authority and dignity. An interview often begins with typical conversation about everyday matters. But it is the goal of the *roshi* to confront the student with the unexpected, to ask a completely unanticipated question, and to provoke a spontaneous response. The master puts obstacles in the student's path to provoke the student to respond spontaneously and not rationally. The student must be taught to abandon intellect for a primal sense.

An example of a *mondo* follows:

> While Rikko, a high government official of the T'ang dynasty, had a talk with his Zen master Nansen, the official quoted a saying of Sojo, a noted monk-scholar of an earlier dynasty:
> "Heaven and earth and I are of the same root, the ten-thousand things and I are of one substance," and continued, "Is not this a most remarkable statement?"
> Nansen called the attention of the visitor to the flowering plant in the garden and said, "People of the world look at these flowers as if they were in a dream." [5]

People do not know how to look at the flowers. It cannot be done as an observer. That is equivalent to dreaming about flowers. In Zen one must share nature's experience: one must *live* nature. To understand the real foundation of existence is to know that humanity and the flowers have a common root. Beauty lies in the meaning it expresses, and this beauty is felt only when the individual ceases being an observer and shares in that meaning.[6]

Perhaps more typically, the *roshi* confronts the disciple with a *koan* like one of the following:

> A monk asked Tung-shan, "Who is the Buddha?" and received the reply: "Three measures of flax."

> A monk asked Hui-neng to reveal the secret of Zen and was asked in turn: "What did your face look like before your parents begot you?" [7]

> A long time ago a man kept a goose in a bottle. How would you remove the goose without hurting it or breaking the bottle?

> Here is a man hanging over a precipice, his teeth clenched in the roots of a tree. His hands are full and his feet cannot quite reach the side of the precipice. Someone leans over and asks him, "What is Zen?" What answer would you make? [8]

Like the *mondo*, the *koan* is enigmatic, jolting us with its irrationality. However, there is a pattern. Some kind of dilemma is posed for the student, some choice among alternatives, all of which are equally impossible. The *koan* represents life itself, in which all the rational alternatives, according to Zen, obscure the truth. The *koan* leads to an impasse.

This can be seen clearly by wrestling with one of the *koans* above. Following Alan Watts' analysis, let us grapple with the goose in the bottle. The goose represents the individual and the bottle the situation. Either the person must abandon the situation in order to be liberated from it, or be crushed by it. However, neither alternative is acceptable. Nothing is to be achieved by abandoning our situation in the world, but nothing is to be gained by being crushed by it either.

One cannot accept either alternative. With that insight, the person experiences *satori*. Suddenly the goose is out of the bottle and the bottle remains unbroken. The individual knows that neither alternative need be accepted. The dilemma has been transcended.

Thus the *mondo* and the *koan* are techniques for pushing through to a whole new awareness of life. Both means require a tremendous intellectual and spiritual struggle, resulting in a complete impasse, and then the realization that every intellectual solution is futile. The "meaning" of either *mondo* or *koan* can never be grasped, because there is no rational meaning to be found. Therefore they present, in miniature, what Alan Watts has called "the giant *koan* of life."

From the standpoint of Zen Buddhism, life itself is a dilemma whose meaning can never be intellectually grasped. So the *mondo* and the *koan* confront the individual with the central problem of life in an intensified way. The disciple must give up intellectual resistance, which demands a rational solution to the meaning of life, and learn to accept life as it is. When the individual can do that, Zen has achieved its purpose.

Satori

The moment of *satori*, or enlightenment, is like opening the windows and doors of the self to let the light stream in. It brings not only a new way of perceiving reality, but also a whole new attitude toward life. Toward this moment disciples strive with great intensity of mind and spirit. Confronted by an intellectual impasse, cornered by the hopelessness of the task, disciples redouble their efforts, concentrating the mind and will for a final assault on the irrationality of *mondo* and *koan*. The will meets the resistance of the enigmatic problem head on, something finally gives way, and *satori* comes. Zen adepts call it, "letting go your hold."

Only primary knowing that comes out of firsthand experience can be claimed as one's own, but primary experience discloses its inner meaning only after a person has exhausted everything belonging to secondary learning. Disciples who come to the end of these resources are ready to make the transition. The Zen view of reality slumbers in every person and awaits an awakening. The awakening is *satori*.

Satori occurs in various degrees. The first time it comes, it will last only a few seconds, but as time goes on the experience becomes more lasting. It is the same in classical meditational practice where the experience of *samadhi* can at first be known for only a few moments. Later the experience returns until the *yogi* can maintain it unbroken for hours. *Satori* becomes more permanent and brings a new way of looking at life and its meaning.

After intense preparation for this moment, *satori* brings enormous relief. But the relief is not the awakening. The relief is temporary and passing; the awakening is the beginning of a lasting view of life and way of living it. After the suddenness of illumination, which some disciples of Zen describe as the great earthquake, what follows is very commonplace and natural: "A sudden clash of thunder, the mind-doors burst open, and lo, there sits the old man (the Buddha-nature) in all his homeliness." [9]

The "uncarved block," the original Buddha-nature of the human individual, has been there all along, but unrecognized for what it is. The person's nature is already the uncarved block; one does not have to do anything to make it so. *Satori* discloses what has been there all along, but the disclosure transforms everything. Nothing has changed, yet nothing can ever be the same again.

A well-known Zen parable makes this point exactly. For those who do not know about Zen, mountains are simply mountains, trees simply trees, and people simply people. During the intensive study of Zen, the disciple learns that all forms are empty, and that the mountains, trees, and people who appear to be real are not at all real. But after *satori*, the mountains are mountains again, the trees trees, and the people people. All things are seen with a new view.

Satori cannot be defined or described. It lies beyond the reach of the intellect. It can be greeted only by silence: the silence of the artist, the mystic, the saint.[10] It is the silence people feel in the presence of great beauty, before the creative power of the universe, in the presence of the holy. Time and space fall away and the world is seen as it really is.

The one in the many and the many in the one

The intellectual side of Zen Buddhism came about in the following way. *Nirvana* is the goal of much Hindu and Buddhist religious practice. It means blowing out the fires of the passions one by one until a state of passionlessness is reached. It is a negative term, and so it did not appeal to the very earthy and practical Chinese spirit. As a result, the conception underwent a transformation. Instead of teaching that *nirvana* was attainable by some kind of yogic withdrawal from life, or nonattachment, Chinese Buddhist thinkers taught that *nirvana* is only attainable in the midst of life *(samsara)*.

Behind this disarmingly simple manner of expression lies some very profound thought. There are two key terms to be mastered, in Chinese *Li* (Japanese, *Ri*) and *Shih* (Japanese, *Ji*). For simplicity, let us use the more common Japanese terms. *Ri* is the *one* running through all things, the existence of which makes the being of all things possible. *Ji* is the *many* things that exist in all their diversity. *Ri* is then the universal, the abstract, the whole, the changeless, while *Ji* is the particular, the concrete, the part, the changing or impermanent.

Ri and *Ji* would appear to be opposite to each other, and poles apart, yet neither can exist without the other. The one *(Ri)* has no form of its own and so it takes form in the many *(Ji)*. However, the many is subject to constant change, cannot exist by itself, and in fact exists only by virtue of the one. Neither can exist without the other. For this state of things as they are, Zen Buddhists use the term *suchness,* the "way-it-is."

This suchness cannot be expressed in words or conceptualized. It must be experienced. It is to experience the one in the many and the many in the one. The one is always taking form in the many, and the many are always pointing beyond themselves to the one. The universe is a never-ending process of interplay between them. Zen thinkers use various analogies to make this interrelatedness and interdependence clear. A favorite is the analogy of a burning candle surrounded by hundreds of mirrors. In the mirrors is reflected not only the light of the candle itself, but also the reflections of all the other mirrors.[11]

All mystics know this experience, however differently they may describe it. It has been expressed classically, in Western terms, by William Blake: "To see a world in a grain of sand/And a heaven in a wild flower/Hold infinity in the palm of your hand/ And eternity in an hour." [12]

This is more than a way of thinking. It represents what happens in the practice of Zen Buddhism. The activity of a Zen center is focused on nature. With loving devotion, the disciple observes the changing of the seasons, the flight of a bird overhead, the spider spinning its web. Nothing in nature is insignificant, not the most commonplace object or occurrence, because even the tiniest fragment of nature contains the whole mystery.

As with mystics everywhere, the knower no longer feels separated from the known. Westerners often regard this as an identification between the person and nature. However, Zen Buddhists do not really believe that one spirit permeates both the human person and nature. It is truer to the spirit of Zen to say Zen Buddhists experience a certain transparency, [13] permitting them to see things as they really are. This leads them to experience nature directly without anything intervening.

This transparency of view discloses that there are not two realities, subject and object. Instead the new way of looking at the world discloses that there never has been a separation of subject and object. This separation is a conception created by the mind. The aim of Zen is to restore the sense of an original inseparability. By *transparency* Zen Buddhists mean clearing away all barriers between ourselves and nature. When the mirror of the mind has been wiped clean, it will reflect the beauty of nature at its truest and best. When this happens, one discovers that everything existing on earth has the same root.

Experiencing nature in Zen terms is not becoming one with it, but learning to live it, to live with it and in it. Zen Buddhists see clearly into the depths of nature, because they live within it and view it from inside. Disciples enter into nature and feel its every pulse. To know a flower, for example, is to enter into the flower, to blossom as the flower, to bask in sunlight, and to feel raindrops on one's petals.[14] To persons viewing its light from within, nature discloses itself and reveals all its secrets. Such persons can feel the life pulsating through them. Seeing into nature in this way leads into the secrets of the flower, which in turn leads into the secrets of the universe, which in turn leads into the secrets of the innermost human self. Self-discovery and the discovery of nature's inmost center go hand in hand.

Harmony with nature

In the technological West the relationship of humanity and nature is often seen as a test of wills. Humanity wrests its livelihood from nature by a battle with the elements, which are seen as antagonistic to, or at the very least uncaring for, human life. Westerners compliment themselves on their conquest of nature and on bending it to their service.

In the homelands of Zen Buddhism, nature has not been seen as an enemy or as an opponent of human life. Nature has been viewed as the great provider and sustainer. All life is rooted in nature, and nature is generous to those who learn to live in harmony with it. Harmony of heaven, earth, and humanity is seen as the highest ideal.

Chinese and Japanese landscape painting is one of the Orient's highest arts, bringing the beauty of nature indoors. However, the subject is nature, not humanity. People and their dwellings are found in such paintings, but they are insignificant when compared with the majesty and beauty of nature. They are not viewed as the culminating achievement of

creation, but as relatively unimportant parts of a
greater harmony.

Toward nature the human individual need have
no other stance than *wu-wei*, the nonaction of "sitting quietly, doing nothing," while "spring comes,
and the grass grows by itself." *Wu-wei* does not so
much mean doing nothing as it means not opposing
the natural way of things. Nature should be permitted to unfold in its own way. Civilization, the
creation of humanity, ought not be allowed to en-
croach upon it.

In pursuing this underlying harmony, Zen Bud-
hists wish to befriend nature. They cannot treat it
as an object for conquest or as something expendable
in the service of humanity. Nature shares life with
people. As their benefactor, it deserves gratitude and
appreciation.

Zen mystics desire to experience nature to the
height of their capacity, *from within.* They wish to
feel nature's changes and rhythms, to *feel* the changing of the seasons, to *feel* the sunrise and the morning. They become completely immersed in contemplation of nature. The Zen monastery is built in close
touch with nature. Those who inhabit it see birds
rocks, moss, and water with new perception.

A hut built for meditation carries out this theme.
The hut is small, thatched with straw, and set deep
among the trees. It is inconspicuous and blends into
its surroundings. In such a setting, the meditator
quickly becomes just another part of nature, like the
birds and insects, the trees and sky.

Nature's mystery is not analyzed or explained
away, it is experienced. In the solitude of meditation, there is bittersweet loneliness. However, the
silence permits one to listen to the deepest sounds
of nature and to plumb its depths. Humility comes

with experiencing nature's all-sufficiency and humanity's relative insignificance.

In the Zen mystical spirit, there is a tendency to see greater meaning in the small and insignificant: the bird's nest, the spider's web, the world of the flea and the mosquito. The majesty of great mountain ranges and the vastness of the ocean may move us to awe, but Zen Buddhists believe that in one humble blade of grass one can hold the whole world of nature in one's hand.

Closeness to nature has its rewards. It brings freedom, naturalness, and spontaneity, freedom in expressing oneself, genuineness, uncalculated responses to persons and to life itself. In possessing these qualities, the human person becomes a channel through which nature's creativity flows.

The Japanese garden

Zen Buddhism has had enormous impact on the cultures of China and Japan. Nowhere is this more apparent than in the arts. Many features of the Eastern artistic tradition owe their inspiration to Zen. In the "one corner" style of painting the artist uses an economy of brush strokes, suggesting rather than overstating or elaborating on the subject. Zen does not explain, it only points the way.

Japanese art, in particular, prizes asymmetry. Zen Buddhists believe they find such asymmetry in nature. Perhaps this is because they view the orderliness of nature as a creation of the human mind, and because it is details in nature in all their uniqueness that are the focus of mystics' attention.

Also valued is *wabi,* which means poverty as a kind of primitive simplicity that is not dependent on wealth and is satisfied with a life close to nature. *Sabi* is also valued. It means loneliness or solitude in the sense of quiet Buddhist detachment. *Yugen* is valued as a mysterious and unknown quality in things that is unfathomable. *Yugen* is a quality lying beneath the surface, providing a glimpse into the changeless in a world of continual change. It is felt in watching the sunset or the flight of wild geese overhead.

It is in the art of the garden that Zen has given the Orient an altogether unique and beautiful tradition. The elements for such a garden are sand, moss, rocks, stone lanterns, water. Most striking are the unusual rocks that appear to grow out of the earth in which they have been buried, just as they would be found in nature. Rocks with unusual forms shaped by wind and water are much treasured, and great pains are taken to find them along the ocean or in mountains.

The garden is intended to be viewed from an open room of the house over a cup of tea. It is not meant to realistically duplicate nature, but rather to suggest nature in the space available. The garden must be perfectly wed with the dwelling, using the available space in such a way that house and garden are an organic unity. Trees and shrubs, rocks and water contribute to the whole. There is a tiny stream whose course is what one would find in nature, with a sand or gravel beach where these elements would be deposited by running water. The origin of the stream is hidden from view. It flows by, and its course winds out of sight. Stepping stones cross the stream and a path leads into the trees. There is the suggestion of following the stream bed to some distant river or following the path wherever it may lead. The garden is suggestive, incomplete, like life itself, inviting viewers to finish it in their own way.

The most famous Zen garden in the world is the stone and sand garden adjoining the Ryonji temple in Kyoto. Built in 1499, it is a rectangle enclosed by a low wall. Within the wall there is only raked sand and fifteen rocks arranged in five groups of three, surrounded in each case by a little moss. It can be viewed only from the meditation platform extending along one side of the temple. Fifteen rocks set in a sea of sand—such a scene poses an obvious question: What does it mean?

Observers who want the garden to represent a scene will perhaps say the rocks are set in a river or that they depict islands in the sea. Japan is, after all, an island kingdom. A common name given Ryonji in Japan is the Garden of the Wading Tiger, implying that the rocks represent a tiger mother and cubs fording a stream.

However, from the standpoint of Zen experience, the symbols are not an attempt to depict any conceivable scene in nature. They are the symbols of contemplation. The sand depicts openness, emptiness. But why the rocks? Because there is no emptiness without form, anymore than there is form without emptiness. *Ri*, the one, the universal, cannot exist withou *Ji*, the many, the particular.[15] The rocks are not isolated. They are buried in the sand. There is an integral relationship between the rocks and sand.

"One corner" painting, asymmetry, poverty, solitude, mystery, and the stone garden, all traits of Japanese artistic taste, are different ways of bringing the beholder to the intuition that "the one is in the many, and the many in the one." Zen Buddhists are completely at home in the universe and see humanity as an integral part of the world. In every way possible, and especially in the arts and the sand and stone garden, Zen Buddhists wish direct contact with life, to the point where they have an altogether new perception of life and themselves.

Chapter 6

Concerns Christians have about the resurgence of religion

Christians cannot conceal some bewilderment about the meaning of the invasion from the East and some concern about certain of its features. Let us discuss one by one the eleven features of Eastern religions described in Chapter 2.

1. A unitary view of the world

Abandoning the two-world conception and holding a more organismic view of the universe is one of the chief marks of the resurgence of religion in the West today. Its sense of a world in which all the parts are interrelated—sun, moon, and stars; seas, atmosphere, and land mass; plants, animals, and humanity—is rightfully viewed as deeply meaningful and satisfying.

But for all of its strength, this view of the world presents concerns for Christians. Such a view readily becomes pantheistic. God is all, and all is God. There is nothing that is not divine. What may well happen then is that God and world, the Creator and the creation, are confused. The world is regarded as divine. By and large, there is little interest on the part of the groups making up the resurgence of religion in the monotheistic God of the Bible. It is the life-force, which is apparent in the rising and the setting of sun and moon, in the courses of the stars and planets, and in the life-cycles of all growing things, that is worshiped as divine.

When the Creator and the creation are so closely identified, and in fact treated as one, two terms for the same reality are no longer needed. When we speak of God *and* the world, one of the terms is superfluous, as Paul Tillich has taught us. The universe itself is regarded as divine, and the term *God* is emptied of its meaning. The conception of God is lost altogether.

Christians are not likely to accept a pantheistic view of God, which denies God's separate existence from the world, and which, by confusing God and the world, denies God's deity.

As deifying nature is pantheism, so deifying natural forces and "sacred" places in nature is polytheism. Few members of the resurgence of religions would deify as the ancients did the storm and the rain, human sexuality and the fertility of flocks and fields, mountain ranges and rivers. Yet there has been a widespread return to ancient polytheistic religious practices.

For example, the following are all being actively practiced today. *Magic* is a way of bringing natural forces under the control of the individual's will. *Incantation* is the use of spells and verbal formulas for the same purpose. *Alchemy* is the "science" of transforming common elements in nature into precious ones (e.g., gold). *Divination* is foreseeing the future by discovering some omen or some other kind of hidden knowledge. *Astrology* is foreseeing the future by charting the influence of the stars and planets on human events. *Spiritualism* is communicating with spirits of the dead. *Necromancy* is learning the future by the help of the spirits of the dead. *Witchcraft* is communicating with evil spirits. *Sorcery* is exercising power over natural forces and events with the help of evil spirits.

What ties this wide spectrum of practices together is that all use natural "powers," the gods and goddesses of the ancient world, to have some human control over the future course of events. That is how polytheism works.

The widespread interest in astrology today affords an apt example. For many people, the practice of astrology represents rebellion against the scientific view of the world, which empties it of human meaning. Astrology becomes a way of affirming that everything in the universe is interrelated, an organic whole, and that human life is a part of the universe's larger meaning.

However, from the Christian standpoint, to submit one's life to the movement of the stars and planets is to subject something which is free, that is, human life, to something which is not free, the determined courses of the stars and planets through the heavens. The difficulty with polytheism, and, in one way or another, with all of the practices above, is that they ignore the real God in favor of deifying some feature or some force in God's world. Polytheism deifies what is less than God, worldly places and forces, and tries to capture the divine in something that can be touched, handled, used, manipulated.

The great strength of biblical monotheism is its insistence that God is one, not many. The Creator is never to be confused with what he has made. To worship worldly forces is to worship the vehicle or medium of God's presence, rather than God. This could hardly be said more clearly than in these words, which will live forever.

> I am the Lord your God. . . . You shall have no
> other gods before me. You shall not make your-
> self a graven image, or any likeness of anything
> that is in heaven above, or that is in the earth
> beneath, or that is in the water under the earth;
> you shall not bow down to them or serve them
> (Exod. 20:2-5).

In an entirely different way, the same point is
made in another famous biblical passage:

> And behold, the Lord passed by, and a great and
> strong wind rent the mountains, and broke in
> pieces the rocks before the Lord, but the Lord
> was not in the wind; and after the wind an
> earthquake, but the Lord was not in the earth-
> quake; and after the earthquake a fire, but the
> Lord was not in the fire; and after the fire a
> still small voice (1 Kings 19:11-12).

Many centuries ago the higher religions displaced the kind of primitive polytheism that is sur-
facing today, and in so doing freed humanity from
subjection to the powers of nature, which had held
people in the ancient world in superstition and fear.
To return to a veneration of those powers in the
20th century is to give up our freedom for an old
slavery. The way to the future cannot lie through
retrogression.

2. A mystical relationship with the world

The mystics of the resurgence of religions cannot
relate to a God distant in the heavens. They want
more direct experience of the divine. It appears that
the desire for such experience is widely felt by contemporary men and women.

In the West God had been defined in very personal
terms. The difficulty with such language is that people may actually come to think of God as a giant
human figure with human characteristics and feel-

ings. Mystics, on the other hand, seek to experience God without seeking a specific definition of God. In fact, mystics will say that God is too great to be described in human language. There are not words or analogies in human speech adequate to contain God. It is an important insight to recognize the greatness of God and the inadequacy of human language to describe him.

However, the end to which the mystical position brings us is very clearly illustrated by the mystical Hindu conception of the divine as *Brahman,* which is described as *neti, neti,* "not-this, not-that." *Brahman* is not defined in qualities it possesses, but rather in terms of what it is not. In addition, *Brahman* is not addressed as "he" or "she," since these pronouns are too personal and concrete, but by the abstract "it." Here a mystical conception of the divine becomes more and more abstract and therefore less and less comprehensible. It is difficult for the worshiper to enter into a personal relationship with a deity so abstract. Finally this abstract conception of God gave way altogether to the nothingness of Buddhist *nirvana.*

In the same way, the resurgence of religions today deals with a mystical conception of the divine so abstract that it is soon emptied of any specific meaning and fades quickly into "cosmic meaning," "world-spirit," or the "cosmic presence." It is a very short step from such a conception of God to no God at all.

Another feature of mystical experience that will concern the Christian is that the God of such experience easily becomes an object. The experience of the mystic's God is the product of the individual's discipline. If the proper steps are followed, the experience of the divine is assured. Such a God is passive and very unlike the God of the Bible, who is the subject who acts, not a passive object who is acted upon.

God can never be passive, or he would not be God. A God who is the predictable outcome of a human religious procedure is not the biblical God, who is free, and acts unpredictably. Luther's way of dealing with this insight was to say, "Let God be God!" Recognize God's majesty and perfect freedom to act. Anything less is to make God too small.

A third concern the Christian will have with mystical practice is its pantheism. The discovery of God in everything—God is all and all is God—is the mystic's remarkable affirmation. It has great clarity and strength. But a God who is everything easily becomes a God who is nothing at all. To say that God is everything identifies divinity with the great diversity of the world and with all pairs of opposites. To say that God is, at one time, both black and white, past and future, east and west, certainly identifies God with all that exists, but it does not tell us very much about divinity. It lacks specific and concrete substance. For God to have an identity, specific characteristics are needed. But the more specific God's characteristics, the less God fits the mystics' needs. Mystics wish to find divinity everywhere, wherever experience leads *them,* and do not desire a God who appears, wherever and whenever *he* wishes.

The Christian's concern about the mystic's God is that it appears to be chiefly the object of the mystic's experience and possesses little identity of its own. Such a God is a pale reflection of the biblical God who acts in history, where least expected, and who is very much in control of the world.

3. Freedom from modern Western materialism

There may be no feature of the resurgence of religion in the West today that rings more true than the conviction that the meaning of life is not to be found in material comforts and possessions. There is a strong tide running against modern technological society and the life-style of material consumption it has created.

The turn away from the material is both a turn inward and a turn toward the more spiritual. Such a movement tends to take people away from the pressures and problems of everyday life, into a private sphere of existence which is peaceful and serene. It can be argued that everyone needs such a sphere as an antidote to the noise and busyness of modern life.

However, there is a difficulty with the retreat from the material into the spiritual, which is illustrated by the culture of India, often considered to be the most "spiritual" on the planet. In Hindu tradition, only the spiritual is considered real, and it is contrasted with the material world of *maya*, the everyday world of time and space, which is considered to be an illusion. As a result, Hindu people do not take the world of matter and space very seriously. The passage of time does not matter very much. People abandon the everyday world, do not respect the realm of matter or take care of it.

The consequences for Indians have often been bitter. Little importance is attached to physical suffering or poor living conditions. Health and hygiene have mattered little. Refuse is thrown into the streets. There are often no sewers to carry waste away, and there is no assured source of clean drinking water.

Indian people expect machines to work, but have little interest in their mysterious working parts. As a result, machines are almost universally abused, rarely properly maintained, often in a condition of exhaustion. People do not understand the machine, do not care to understand it, do not respect what it can do, and do not take care of it. It belongs to the world of illusion, after all.

It is not likely that Westerners will forsake the machine world, but there is implicit in the desire to transcend the material world a subtle contempt for it, which does not bode well for the future. Contempt for the material world will not help solve the urgent problems of modern society: industrial pollution, urban decay, energy exhaustion, chronic poverty, widespread crime, worldwide spread of lethal weapons, etc. The material world, or the secular, is the base on which the spiritual, or the sacred, exists. To abandon the material world in order to experience spiritual realities would be to cut the root upon which both worlds are dependent for their existence.

4. Many paths to the truth

The many paths to the truth being taken today are meeting the varied needs of pluralistic Western society. Each person may find personal truth without sacrificing individuality. The climate in which this happens is not only tolerant of diversity, but it also encourages individuals to make their own way without relying on the guidance of others. Tolerance is a laudable ideal, and whatever contributes to understanding and acceptance of people by others deserves our support.

However, the present pluralistic climate also indicates that Westerners have lost their center. In place of a single truth, there are now many truths existing side by side. This may also be called relativism. No single truth is regarded as absolute. All truths, however different from one another, are regarded as possessing some truth.

This will concern Christians, because the one truth is denied to make room for many truths. And among the many truths there is much that Christians find unworthy of acceptance. Whenever all truths are considered true, nothing is altogether true, because everything is true in part. For Christians, this appears to put the truth of God in Jesus Christ in jeopardy.

To complicate the situation, not only is the cultural climate in the West pluralistic and relativistic, it is also syncretistic. *Syncretism* is the amalgamation of ideas and practices that come from different sources and do not really belong together. There is much syncretism in the present resurgence of religion. People draw insights and practices together from the most diverse sources if they promise to answer their needs. Eastern and Western practices flow together. Modern psychotherapeutic procedures are held side by side with Hindu or Buddhist meditational practices. Some of the most lofty religious principles ever given expression by humanity are held together with some of the most gross and crude practices of primitive magic and superstition. To be syncretistic in this sense is not to be discriminating.

An example may be drawn from Asian Buddhism. Buddhist tolerance is understood in such a way that it coexists with other religious practices rather than displacing them. The theory is that Buddhism's truth is superior to all other forms of truth and that that superiority will eventually become clear to all. And the theory is attractive. But in practice Buddhist ideas and ideals do not always succeed in proving their superiority. Just as often primitive superstitions draw the individual down to their level.

In much of southern Asia, Buddhism coexists with a worship of primitive spirits called *nats*. The spirits are said to possess the land, haunt it, and they must be placated with offerings. People do not fear the Buddha, for he has been dead for 25 centuries, but they fear the *nats,* who are very much alive and can be malicious if not venerated properly. Buddhism has not conquered the *nats;* the latter are key features of the living, day-to-day religion of the people. Buddhism is a remote scheme of meanings beyond most people's reach.

The trouble with syncretism is that nothing is true because everything is true. Because there is no single truth, many people today drift from one set of religious meanings to another, sampling one truth after another. Infatuated with one of the new cults influenced by the Orient, they throw themselves into it, only to discover its weaknesses and later abandon it. They pass, like Argonauts, from one imagined haven to another.

It is a terrible thing to live without a center. Everyone needs a single truth around which to orient life. It is one of the marks of our times that people feel fragmented, pulled in all directions by the competing forces and influences of modern life. A single truth means wholeness, where every truth takes its place in relationship with all other truths in an overarching design.

5. The promise of altering human consciousness

That humanity is in need of change and that religion exists to help it reach its highest potential can hardly be denied. The new resurgence of religion would not be taking place if it did not promise a radical transformation to many people today.

As important as this is, Christians will be concerned about the unjustified optimism about humanity underlying many of the "new religions." It contains elements of the West's 19th-century faith in the innate goodness of people, the inevitability of human progress, and the inherent improvability of human character. This preoccupation with humanity and its potential is combined with the Eastern belief that humanity can be initiated into hidden worlds of experience beyond everyday life. Together they create a climate in which men and women expect to develop themselves without limitation. Christians will be concerned that this transformation is expected to take place solely on the basis of human action, without the activity of God.

There is a second concern Christians will have with the focus on human capacity for transformation. Turning inward is a turning away from the world of society and its problems. Fellow humans and their claims upon one are ignored. The entire process of cultivating one's individual potential and the spiritual dimensions of one's character is self-centered. In fact, the present concern with the self represents a desire to escape modern industrial society.

But problems do not disappear because men and women evade them by turning in upon themselves. In fact, one of Christianity's best insights is that no real development of the self is possible except in relationship with other persons and the larger problems of society and community. Preoccupation with the self often inhibits its development, while giving oneself unselfishly to causes that take one outside the self is the path to real development of one's potential. Self-realization takes place not in isolation, but in relationship with persons and problems.

This observation brings us to a related concern. The "new religions" have little ethical or moral content. Emphasis is on self-growth according to an accepted discipline or *sadhana*. But the discipline, however detailed its instructions and however difficult it

may be to follow, is not concerned with ethical or
moral issues. Does religion not require the limitation
of the person's self-interest out of consideration for
God and the well-being of other people? For how
long can religious forms that involve preoccupation
with the self, that ignore social issues, and that have
no ethical content, continue to nurture spiritual life?

6. Direct rather than secondary experience

Coming to know something for oneself is always
better than secondary knowing. Spontaneous and
creative religious experience holds the promise of
revitalizing a stultifying religious life of ritual and
habit.

However, Christians will be concerned on several
counts with the emphasis on experience. First, from
the Christian point of view, *direct* experience of God
is not possible. God can be experienced in all creation and in the historical process. God's presence and
activity can be discovered in divine revelation to
humanity. However, it is not possible for God to be
known directly and remain God. God cannot become
the object of human experience and remain God.
God is the divine subject who acts in and upon the
world, who can never be the object of human activity. So while women and men can directly experience God's world and works, they cannot have a
direct experience of God.

Secondly, religious people draw strength from
God, in whom their lives are rooted. Not only do
they draw sustenance from God as the ground of
their being, but they acknowledge their dependence
and reliance upon God. However, personal religious
experience is self-centered and shifts the interest
from God the giver to humanity the experiencer. The
emphasis falls on the content of the experience. The

change in emphasis is often very subtle, but the focus is no longer on God who gives, but on the experience as the possession of the individual.

The mysticism of the medieval world, with its promise of an intimate and transforming experience of God, attracted Martin Luther. But as congenial as it was to his spirit, he was finally suspicious of it. His insight into religious meaning did not rest on ecstatic experience, but rather on a new understanding of the Bible. It was of great importance to him that his insight was not made valid by the effect which it had on his inner self. In that his insight was drawn from the Bible's message, it possessed a certain objective character. If instead the insight relied solely on his subjective experience, it was open to the widest difference of interpretation. Luther believed the inner world of humanity to be a complicated labyrinth from which it was difficult, if not impossible, to return with a certain and reliable truth. Most products of human experience are colored by individuals' imagination and serve their self-interest.

One of the problems with direct experience, then, is that it has no objective validity and may be made out by individuals to be anything they wish. People can become lost in their own subjectivity in such a way that they lose all certainty as to what is true. Only some standard of objectivity can restore that lost certainty.

Thirdly, Christians will be concerned that people desiring a certain intensity of religious experience may easily confuse the methods they use with their goals. From the Christian point of view, the goal to be desired is a rich relationship with God. The actual content of the experience and the methods of religious discipline used are much less important. However, many members of the new religions seem to belong to a cult of experience. In their quest for an intensity of religious experience, they can easily become interested primarily in the experience for the experience's sake.

Running through these concerns is a common thread which in effect says that the focus on experience is misplaced. The focus is better directed to the God who is the source of all human life and experience.

7. A specific program of spiritual discipline

Little spiritual growth can take place without spiritual discipline. Lack of spiritual discipline is one of the reasons for spiritual anemia in traditional Western religions today. However, Christians may become concerned with the emphasis on discipline to the exclusion of other features of the spiritual life.

Christian theology teaches that no spiritual discipline, however active and strenuous, can lead to God. No spiritual ladders can be built from earth to heaven. No human action can discover the route to God. God is never the object of human ingenuity and discovery. The route between God and humanity leads *from* God, is always taken at God's initiative, because of God's *grace*. The conception of grace is the central concept of Christian faith. It contrasts the activity of women and men and the activity of God. The first chapter of Romans makes clear that the unaided religious quest of humanity leads to the deification of human forms and the deification of natural forces, but it cannot lead to the living God. Only God can disclose God.

Secondly, spiritual discipline, without grace, can be a very heavy burden to bear. Christians have had a very long historical experience with religion as law. Discipline, as law, places all responsibility for success or failure on individuals, and frequently this weight of responsibility is more than they can bear. The discipline required by many of the new religions is very demanding, and those failing to keep it are condemned by their failure.

Discipline, without grace, is simply a form of legalism, and no form of legalism can ever free the human spirit. Only grace can do that. From the Christian point of view there is no point in adopting Eastern religious practices that fail to liberate the human person. This would be to exchange willingly one's freedom for a form of slavery.

Thirdly, many who adopt a religious discipline want a certain personal status and view their exertions as a way of achieving spiritual power over others and over the world. In India the ascetic who sacrifices normal food, clothing, and shelter is viewed as one who renounces power of one kind to achieve power of another sort. Renunciation of the normal necessities of everyday life is seen not as a loss, but as a way of exercising control, and therefore power, over the environment. Ascetics are widely believed to possess powers of omniscience, the power to work miracles, the power of clairvoyance, the power to transport themselves spiritually to remote portions of the earth, and occult powers of various kinds.

Many who are attracted by Oriental religions envision such powers. Beyond self-control, they desire control over others and even over the natural forces of the universe by the possession of advanced states of consciousness. The powers sought are not subject to the normal ideals of morality. In fact, the person who attains them is generally considered to be beyond good and evil and therefore not subject to society's standards for proper behavior.

Christians are justifiably concerned by any exercise of power over others and over the world that is not subject to the control morality is expected to exercise. It can be argued that religion exists to temper the selfish human exercise of power by a deepened sense of the human community. Christians, who are themselves far from perfect, would like to point the individual bent on acquiring such psychic powers to the example of Jesus of Nazareth, who submerged his own ego's needs in the greater human good.

8. Prayer becomes meditative and contemplative

Prayer that is merely petitional can easily become superficial and stand in the way of a meaningful relationship with God. It can cheapen the relationship and reduce God to little more than a cosmic Santa Claus. In spite of this fact, Christians are concerned by any definition of the relationship between God and humanity that denies or reduces its personal character.

There is an important difference between East and West at this point. Biblical religion considers personal individuality to be of the highest value, while Eastern religion moves beyond the self to a kind of impersonality. Christians have a deep conviction about the value of the individual human personality, which derives from the biblical teaching that it is the highest product of the creativity of God. They believe that their individuality is their uniqueness and the most precious thing there is about them. By contrast, in Hindu tradition the individual self is something to be overcome in the all-inclusive, impersonal reality of *Brahman*. Buddhism carries this logic a step further by teaching that the existence of the individual self is an illusion to be overcome. Either way, the relationship between humanity and the greater reality is not personal.

Whenever practices of meditative and contemplative prayer substitute an impersonal relationship for a personal one, something very precious is lost from the Christian point of view. In the creative purposes of God, personal individuality is the highest form of being in the universe. If this is so, the highest forms of relationship are also personal, and any relationship that is less than personal is less than the highest. A relationship with God must then be a relationship between divine and human persons. Any loss of the personal character of this relationship makes either God or humanity less than personal. When this happens, it is no longer possible to speak of a relationship between them that is loving and requires responsibility. Christians oppose any denial of personal relationship with God.

There is another problem with meditative and contemplative practice. Many mystics do not hold a clear and unambiguous view of the divine reality with which they hope to relate. The end result of their experience is then really an enriched relationship with the self. Freed from all distractions of the earth, individuals move toward their own center, overcoming all alienation from the self. The result is called *integration* in many classical scriptures of India, the self united with the self. However useful this experience may be, it is communion with the self and nothing more, if no relationship with God follows.

Christians, then, believe prayer involves a relationship of giving and receiving such as persons share. For them the impersonal nature of much meditative and contemplative practice is an impoverishment of what prayer can be.

9. Cultivating the bodily dimension of life

The current emphasis on the bodily side of religious experience is one of the best and most needed features of the resurgence of religion. Yoga and fasting; meditation, exercise, and physical fitness; and a diet of natural foods with vegetarian eating prominent, are all welcome antidotes to many of the ills of modern civilization. And helpful as they may be to the individual, their greatest significance lies in their contribution to a "holistic" view of the human person. The need for such a holistic approach, as illustrated by current trends in medicine and psychotherapy, is clear. It is therefore difficult to take issue with any feature of such an important trend.

However, Christians are concerned about how this emphasis is applied. In the West today the desire for an intense bodily experience dominates and therefore obscures other human needs. People are weary of words and intellectual descriptions and want to pursue experience as an end in itself.

As a corrective to neglecting the body, this trend is valid. However, people frequently want to try everything, and because no sensate experience can satisfy for long, they turn from one experience to another. This means that any quest for an intensity of experience is bound to fail in the end. Bodily experiences soon grow repetitious and lose their capacity to satisfy. The person desiring such experiences is driven to ever new dimensions of sensation. The search tyrannizes the victim.

This persistent problem plagues many today. They move from cult to cult, from one promise of altered states of consciousness to another, and from one emotional high to another. Those who know the movement best testify to this continual instability.

There is about the quest an anxiety, even an air of desperation, which continues to push the serenity so eagerly sought just out of reach.

Perhaps the most damning criticism that can be brought to bear against cultivating the bodily dimension of life is that it can easily deny the very holistic approach to life it was meant to strengthen. If the pursuit of sensory experience is undertaken in a subtly anti-intellectual way, it can deny the importance of mind and thought, and of religious insight and spirit, and can easily prove self-defeating. A holistic approach to life requires activity of the mind, spirit, and body in a balanced and meaningful relationship.

10. A guide to the realm of the spirit

Earlier we referred to Max Weber's distinction between *emissary* and *exemplary* religious leadership. Emissary leaders, like the great prophets of Israel, address an authoritative, divine word to the human situation. Exemplary leaders, on the other hand, teach by example. They are often called charismatic, in the strict meaning of the term, "gifted." The resurgence of religion abounds with exemplary leaders, gurus, roshis, strong, dominating persons, often said to possess occult powers. They are the strong allies required by those who want to invade the inner world and deal successfully with its obstacles and difficulties.

As useful as a spiritual master may be, dangers in the relationship will concern Christians. Disciples must venerate the master and cooperate fully. If the desired spiritual changes are to take place, the disciple must submit to the master. As the disciple's ego diminishes, dependence on the master grows. These strong personalities exercise enormous control over their disciples. As in all forms of therapy, the disciple/patient is highly vulnerable to the master/therapist's suggestion. This places far-reaching control over one person's destiny in another person's hands.

The master needs superior awareness and spiritual discrimination. It is not enough to gain mastery of subject-matter. Insight into the disciple's inner needs and knowledge into how to meet them is required. While the master may appear to be devoid of ambition in all the usual ways having to do with food and shelter and material well-being, he really desires supreme power. Having renounced power and status in the outer world, the master desires spiritual power and status, power over other person's minds and their inner destinies.

In the East, religion was never intended to be for the masses. Spiritual wisdom is so precious that it is to be given only to those who show themselves worthy and who are willing to use it in the right way. To receive it, people must be willing to make any sacrifice, so that nothing stands between them and the truth. Eastern religion is thus esoteric. Knowledge is power, and the master holds great power in his ability to give or deny knowledge to any individual.

Disillusioned with traditional forms of Western religious life and still searching for the meaning of human existence, many people today fall under the influence of a spiritual master. In a troubled time, when all the presuppositions of Western culture are being challenged and when it seems impossible to believe in previously accepted religious beliefs, the appeal of an authoritarian figure can be overwhelming. We are undergoing what the historians call "a failure of nerve." The old certainty that Western civilization has all the answers and has much to teach the rest of the world is shaken. There is danger that in a difficult time, Westerners should all too readily put themselves in the hands of an authoritarian figure who makes all the decisions in his disciples' lives. Many parents whose young people have been programmed by such masters and led away from home and into unusual and sometimes undesirable life-styles, will testify to the danger.

11. Living harmoniously with nature

The widespread desire to recover a sense of harmony with nature is one of the great strengths of the current resurgence of religion. Christians can and will applaud its influence. However, there are also concerns.

Traditionally the West has been life- and history-affirming, while the East has been more resigned to life and nature. Underlying this difference are totally dissimilar views of time. In the biblical tradition, time is the good gift of God, and, because it is full of creative possibility, it is liberating. In the East, the universe is regarded as without beginning or end, and an individual human life is no more than a brief moment in the vast sweep of time. In such a view, time weighs heavily on the individual, who can only be resigned to it.

Westerners are expansive about the degree to which conditions on the earth can be changed. They accept few limits on the expression of their human capacity to leave the earth a very different place than they found it. They have deep cultural faith in the saving character of change, and the courage to try anything. This determination not to be resigned to intolerable conditions and to change what can be changed, has led to significant advances for the race.

In the East, time's expanse is so vast, there is little likelihood that anything humanity might do could leave much of a mark on it. So rather than being intent on changing things, the people of Asia have traditionally sought harmony between themselves and nature. Where harmony is the goal, humanity recognizes the limits placed on its self-expression and seeks to find its place in a larger design. The Western view has great faith in history and change; the Eastern takes comfort in nature and its recurrence.

Contemporary Westerners, however, are disillusioned about their ability to radically change the historical world, and many wish to turn to the harmonics of nature. In turning from the historical world to nature's rhythm and recurrence, people declare their desire for continuity instead of revolutionary change, for stability instead of anarchy, for order instead of chaos. The natural promises a secure haven from the stormy seas of historical change.

However, from the Christian point of view, there could be no greater tyranny than to be confined to nature and to be resigned to the eternal recurrence of its cycles. Then time would weigh heavily on life: ceaseless, directionless change; nothing enduring, nothing eternal; no purpose, no meaning for human life. And nature's final word is the slow dying of autumn and the final death of winter.

Sensitive to the desire to return to nature, Jean Paul Sartre and Albert Camus taught an entire generation of Westerners to abandon the biblical view of time and to accept the alternative view of recurrence. Their advice to Westerners was to "unlearn to hope." They led many Westerners to give up any design for human progress and any hope for a better world. However, for Christians to "unlearn to hope" would be equivalent to denying their faith in God, the divine creative design for the world, and their own humanity.

In the great creation accounts in Genesis, both animals and humans belong to nature, but what distinguishes them is the gift to humanity of the *image of God* (Gen. 1:26). This gift of a spiritual nature contains within it the possibility for creative change. With its animal nature, humanity belongs to nature and its recurrence; with its spiritual nature, it belongs to history and the possibility of progress toward a better future.

To return to nature is only going back to humanity's animal self, to the experience of the senses and to the drives of instinct. To accept confinement to animal life is to deny the Creator's most precious gift, human freedom and the capacity for transcendence of nature.

Christianity offers salvation from the cycle of nature. The biblical dimension of hope rests firmly on its concept of God. God is possibility; God is tomorrow; God is the future; God is that unpredictable creativity that has not yet been disclosed. God is the promise of the creatively new. The creation of the universe is not simply a past event that occurred millions of years ago. Creation has not ceased. It goes on in the present, in all of the creatively new events of each new day.

Christians are reluctant to return to nature, unless it leads to rediscovering nature's God. If the return does lead to that rediscovery, a reaffirmation of Christian hope will follow. "The creation itself will be set free from its bondage to decay and obtain the glorious liberty of the children of God" (Rom. 8:21).

Chapter 7

What Christians can learn from the resurgence of religion

What can Christians learn from the invasion from the East and how should they react? Many Christians are bewildered. Is Christianity failing to meet some need in Western life which can be better met by Eastern religious ideas and practices? That would appear to be the meaning of the success the resurgence of religion is having. If so, perhaps Christians can learn some things from it.

God has not left himself without a witness in the great religious traditions of Asia, which inform so large a part of the human family. Perhaps they can lead us to rediscover dimensions of meaning in the Christian faith that have been long neglected and ignored.

1. A unitary view of the world

Certainly the widespread desire for a more unitary and organismic view of the universe is valid and healthy. It provides people with a more meaningful and satisfying world view than the Age of Science has created.

However, Christians have a contribution to make that can greatly enrich this emphasis. Christians

can confidently proclaim their faith in the one God
who stands at the center of their scheme of meaning. Because the resurgence of religion is strongly
pluralistic, and even polytheistic, it has done little
to affirm the existence of the one God at the center
of reality. But, people cannot live for long without a
center for their lives.

Fragmentation is one of the marks of modern
Western society. People are pulled in a multiplicity
of directions by powerful and often contradictory
forces. With one segment of their lives they act pro-
fessionally, with another they vote their political
convictions, with another they relate with their families, and with another they hold their religious and
moral convictions. While each of these roles may be
perfectly satisfying in itself, the problem is putting
them together in some meaningful way. Without a
center, that is very difficult to do, and many men and
women never achieve real unity in their lives. Ideally
each segment of life should make its contribution
to the whole, and an individual's experience become
unified around an integrating center. There is no
stronger center than faith in the one God, Creator
and Lord of the heavens and the earth.

A second response Christians can make is to emphasize a more mystical conception of God in keep-
ing with the current aim. The long, rich tradition
of Christian mysticism can and should be recovered.
Rather than a divine being remote in the heavens,
an all-powerful supernatural force above and beyond the world, in the mystical tradition God is the
ground of all being. St. Augustine voices that tradition in these memorable words:

> What place is there in me into which my God
> can come, who made heaven and earth? Is there
> anything in me, O Lord my God, that can con-
> tain you? . . . Or should I not rather say, that I

> could not exist unless I were in you, from whom
> are all things, by whom are all things, in whom
> are all things? [1]

The mystical doctrine of God does not emphasize his supernatural isolation above and beyond the world, but rather divine presence and activity in every corner of the natural world. Nothing could exist without being rooted in God's being. From the mystical perspective, God did not once and for all create all that exists, but is actively creating in each new day. God is present in all creativity: in the birth of every child, in the fertility of every farmer's field, in the birth of every great idea and every solution for difficult social problems, in the laboratory of the scientist, in the classroom of the teacher, in industry and commerce. Wherever there is creativity there is God.

However, while proclaiming a more mystical concept of God, Christians will not want to lose God's personal character. Where Western religions have traditionally defined God in very personal terms, Eastern religions have tended to view ultimate reality in a more abstract way. A God who is viewed with all too human characteristics becomes the old grandfather in the sky of popular conception, while a God who is viewed as pure abstraction becomes increasingly incomprehensible and is lost finally in nothingness. Christianity possesses the resources to strike a balance between these emphases.

2. A mystical relationship with the world

In the long history of humanity, three different forms of mystical consciousness have emerged. They represent three different kinds of union: that of the self with nature, that of the self with the self, and that of the self with God.[2]

The first is nature mysticism in which mystics experience kinship with everything they see. They enjoy the sheer beauty of the earth: in land, mountains, and sea; in sunrise and sunset; in golden grain, azure water, green valleys, and bold gray mountains. They are moved to awe and they experience a sense of unity with the greater world.

In the second mystical stage, mystics long for a higher plane of experience. Freed from all distraction, they seek a higher state of consciousness in quiet and isolation. They move toward their center, toward the ground of their existence. In this state of contemplation, the self overcomes all alienation from itself. The mystics of the East call this *integration,* the union of the self with the self.

However, Christian mysticism has a still higher path to offer. In this third stage, the individual enters into a personal relationship with God. What makes this experience unique is that God's action now takes the place of all human activity. All the human self can do is surrender, not act, but receive. The mystic can give God nothing, but only take what God bestows.

In this rich experience of God's nature, Christian mysticism has much to offer a weary world that has gone as far as its own effort can take it. The promise of God's presence in a world otherwise empty and devoid of meaning is balm for contemporary souls. It can also lead adherents of Eastern religions to a higher state of mystical awareness.

3. Freedom from modern Western materialism

Christians need not follow the lead of the Buddha to deplore the material entanglements of property and possessions. There was a strong disregard for material possessions in the preaching of Jesus.

> Fear not, little flock, for it is your Father's good
> pleasure to give you the kingdom. Sell your pos-
> sessions, and give alms; provide yourselves with
> purses that do not grow old, with a treasure in
> the heavens that does not fail, where no thief
> approaches and no moth destroys. For where
> your treasure is, there will your heart be also
> (Luke 12:32-34).

The disciples, like their Lord, were expected to separate themselves from their families, remove themselves from all responsibilities to society in the usual
sense (Matt. 10:34-39, 8:21-22) and dispose of their
property. Indeed, they "left all" to follow him.

The communal life of the early Christians described in the Book of Acts was an outgrowth of the
practice of Jesus and his disciples. Poverty was to
be banished among Christians through the equal dis-
tribution of wealth. The right of private property
was voluntarily given up and provision for the needs
of all made through sale of one's property and dedication of the proceeds to the common good.

> Now the company of those who believed were of
> one heart and soul, and no one said that any of
> the things which he possessed was his own, but
> they had everything in common. . . . There was
> not a needy person among them, for as many as
> were possessors of lands or houses sold them,
> and brought the proceeds of what was sold and
> laid it at the apostles' feet; and distribution was
> made to each as any had need. (Acts 4:32,
> 34-35).

Christians then need not look to other traditions
for inspiration in simplifying life and finding liberation from the thralldom of acquisition and possession. That this Christian practice requires rediscovery, however, is proof that the ideology of private property, investment, and profit has effectively
buried it from sight in the capitalist West. In order
to respond to the resurgence of religion on this issue, Christians need only rediscover their own birth-

right. If they do so, they will learn again that less is more, that material possessions cannot guarantee security, and that serenity of life follows necessarily from following Jesus' advice.

4. Many paths to the truth

In our study of Hinduism we noted that four spiritual paths *(margas)* exist side by side in Indian life to offer alternative ways for people with different temperaments to follow. There is implied in this arrangement the recognition that different people have different spiritual needs.

By contrast in the West, Christians have been less catholic than Hindus and have tended to talk in terms of "one way." Exclusivism, a sense of chosenness, and the conviction that they alone possessed the truth combined to create an intolerant attitude in the Christian West. The monotheism of Moses was achieved by excluding all the gods of the ancient Middle East except one. In India monotheism did not come about in this way, but by assimilating the qualities of different gods into the one God.[3] The result is that there is room, within this one system of belief, for differing religious positions to exist side by side without inconsistency or conflict. Conformity is forced upon no one; the word heretic does not exist. Different spiritual paths lead to the same spiritual end.

Christians are capable of the same tolerance. In addition, Christians can provide for a greater diversity of needs among their people. In the *Bhagavad Gita* the four paths are *karma-yoga,* the way of action; *jnana-yoga,* the way of insight and understanding; *bhakti-yoga,* the way of personal devotion to and relationship with God; and *raja-yoga,* the way of rigorous spiritual discipline. While such a scheme is obviously not normative for Christians, it is suggestive, and if Christians were to use something like it, the results might look like this.

Christians who chose the *way of action* would commit themselves to serve in the area of social concern. Their sphere of action might well take them to the city, to the streets, to a downtown soup kitchen supported by area congregations. Such Christians would be concerned with the application of the biblical message to current social and political issues.

Christians who chose the *way of learning* would make the congregation a forum for discussion again, a place for hard intellectual work. For most of its history, the interior of the synagogue, from which the form of the congregation originally sprang, resembled the reading room of a library more than a place of worship in our modern sense. The Christian community could become a place where theology *is made* and a forum for significant discussion again.

Christians who chose the *way of personal devotion* would seek a rich relationship with God and with other people both inside and outside the congregation. It may be for them to adapt to modern life some of the communal forms used in the early church and described in the Book of Acts.

Christians who chose the *way of spiritual discipline* would want to practice the presence of God. They would need the support of the congregation in creating the right environment and in adopting a suitable discipline. The spiritual depth of such experience can be an effective antidote to many of the anxieties and strains of contemporary life.

By making a greater diversity of spiritual paths available for their people, Christians can meet a broader spectrum of needs. Every person will be able to find something meaningful out of the rich variety of paths available.

5. The promise of altering human consciousness

To help people achieve altered consciousness, Christians can create, more than they have done in the past, a community dedicated to the development of the selfhood of its people.

Most disciples of Eastern religious forms, when they discuss inner transformation, describe it as "transcending" the world around them. They desire "higher states of consciousness," *bhavana,* cultivation of mental states, and *samadhi,* meditative trance. Christians can point them to a whole new awareness of their potential as sons and daughters of God and to methods for the realization of that potential.

There is no higher human destiny than growing into the image of God. This vital process of discovering the divine purpose for the individual is aided by all kinds of experiences, but none more important than relationships with other people, good friends, teachers, a close family. Christians can provide the environment of a loving and supportive family or community in which that process can unfold.

Secondly, Christians have a powerful resource in the person of their Lord. Human personality grows and develops best by imitation. In fact, people's ideals and models are the clearest indication of the direction in which they will develop. For this reason the quality of the models chosen is vital.

In the Eastern tradition the spiritual master provides that model. In Christianity, the example of Jesus' struggle for selfhood can serve as a guide. However, what is needed is the humanity of Jesus serving as a model for the humanity of his people. It is not Jesus as some kind of cosmic or supernatural figure who can help. He must be understood as a person of flesh and blood, with hopes and fears like the Christian's own. He must be seen as a person who struggled to know who he was and what the will of God was for him.

As Christians rediscover how Jesus' selfhood emerged out of his struggle with life, with his generation, and with the will of God for him, they will find strength for meeting the challenges of their lives in the 20th century. Then perhaps the hope of St. Paul will be realized: "We are to grow up in every way ... into Christ ... (to) attain ... to mature manhood, to the measure of the stature of the fulness of Christ" (Eph. 4:15, 13).

However, none of this can begin to take place without a new doctrine of humanity that makes room for a theology of human self-development. The main barrier is traditional Augustinian-Lutheran pessimism about humanity. The doctrine of original sin and the concept of human depravity have contributed much to this pessimism. Good theology it may be, but it is not very good psychology. Tell people often enough that they are mean, perverse, and depraved, and you can hardly blame them for acting mean, perverse, and depraved. On the contrary, if you teach them the equally biblical insights that they have been created in the image of God, that they have been made a "little less than God," that they have been "crowned with glory and honor," and that they have been given dominion over the earth, they will try to measure up to that image. You bring out the best there is in people by challenging them to reach for the highest of which they are capable.

6. Direct rather than secondary experience

The widespread desire for new, immediate, powerful, and deep religious experience has not been met by the Christian community on the whole. To those who represent the new consciousness, mainline churches seem characterized by moralism and verbalism. Their lack of an ecstatic dimension coupled with what appears to be a prejudice against impulsive, spontaneous religious experience has led to the disaffection of those who belong to the new movement.[4]

Joseph Needleman has captured this disaffection accurately in the following description:

> It is as though millions of people suffering from a painful disease were to gather together to hear someone read a textbook of medical treatment in which the means necessary to cure their disease were carefully spelled out. It is as though they were all to take great comfort in that book and in what they heard, going through their lives knowing that their disease could be cured, quoting passages to their friends, preaching the wonders of this great book, and returning to their congregation from time to time to hear more of the inspiring diagnosis and treatment read to them. Meanwhile, of course, the disease worsens and they eventually die of it, smiling in grateful hope as on their deathbed someone reads to them yet another passage from the text. Perhaps for some a troubling thought crosses their minds as their eyes close for the last time: "Haven't I forgotten something? Something important? Haven't I forgotten actually to undergo treatment?"[5]

The charismatic movement has tried to reintroduce the dimension of ecstatic experience into the Christian community. However, it has often made such experience normative, to the exclusion of other dimensions of the spiritual life, alienating many Christians.

How can Christians respond more creatively to the desire for primary experience in the contemporary situation? In seeking primary experience, they must maintain a proper relationship to the Word of God. Luther saw clearly that objective and subjective factors must be balanced. The *objective* factor that balances primary experience is the Bible, stamped with the authority of God. While God has not confined divine activity to biblical revelation, God is revealed to humanity through the message contained in the Word. All Christian religious experience must be measured by its criteria.

The difficulty with the Bible is that when it tells us about what God has done in the lives of Moses or Jeremiah or Jesus, it is "words about" what happened; it is not the experience itself. A book is, by its very nature, a verbal way of conveying religious truth. It is necessarily made up of words, phrases, sentences, and paragraphs on pages.

A second complication is that a book is the finished product of a moment of experience or creativity from the past. The original experience was fresh and spontaneous. But as such original moments pass, their content is conserved, recorded, and passed on to successive generations. What was a primary experience of the presence of God for Jeremiah, can at best be only secondary experience for today's Christian.

The same deficiency of secondary compared with primary experience can be seen in Christian worship. For today's disciples of Eastern religious practices, traditional worship seems to have lost much of its spontaneity and the power to transform its participants. It has all become rather stereotyped and predictable. The script is all worked out in advance, and the parts are all known. The whole exchange is rather tame.

But what of the *subjective* factor? Christians must so enter into the worlds of King David or of Jesus, that they become their own, and they can share the primary experience of God those great figures encountered. The record of God's activity contained in the Bible is a dead word until it is made alive in Christians' living experience. God's activity in history is not confined to the period from 1300 B.C. to A.D. 100. God is not dead. Christians must experience the creative presence of God in the unfolding events of today. They need to rediscover an air of expectancy, looking and waiting with anticipation for the activity of God in all the unexpected corners of this world.

To move from secondary to primary experience is to leave the tried and the tired behind and to search anew for the presence of God with freshness and spontaneity. Those who seek in new ways will find. And new experience of God possesses a revolutionary power that can have tremendous impact on Christians. As in the early days of Christian history, it has the power to turn the world upside down, to radically transform Christian life and the world. Such power is by no means beyond Christians' reach when *objective* and *subjective* factors find their proper balance.

7. A specific program of spiritual discipline

Søren Kierkegaard, with typical unerring insight, wrote:

> There was a time when one could almost be afraid to call himself a disciple of Christ, because it meant so much. Now one can do it with complete ease, because it means nothing at all (*Journals*, 1851).

By and large, traditional Christian religious forms are marked today by an absence of practical discipline. The Sunday morning worship service, which unfortunately is the extent of most Christians' involvement in religious practice, does not provide them with the daily discipline which deeply influences their vocational performance and transforms their lives.

The success the Asian religious practices have had in providing specific discipline for modern Westerners is evidence that many people feel the need for such discipline. In our permissive age, where there are few landmarks and guideposts, people long for religious discipline and the inner transformation it promises.

One of the most tragic marks of Western religious life today is the gap between belief and practice. If Christians actually did what their message says should be done, they would be taken more seriously by their critics and their communities would prove much more attractive to people outside their ranks.

Grace is what God does; discipleship is what Christians do. Discipleship means following Christ. It cannot mean less than self-renunciation, freedom from possessions and prejudice, bearing a part of the suffering of others, being merciful and compassionate. But such lofty values need specific discipline to make them concrete. One Christian congregation expresses this concern in four central convictions:

> First, that the service of God requires total commitment. Second, that power demands discipline. Third, that the gift of the Holy Spirit depends upon the existence of a true fellowship. . . . Fourth, that such Christian fellowship is best assured in a small group. . . .

The Christian is to be "engaged simultaneously in contemplative spiritual disciplines and in active mission at some point of the world's needs." [6]

Contemplative discipline and active service represent the two sides of the Christian life. Typical Westerners can only begin the first by creating a daily quiet time devoted to the spiritual side of their

being. An environment must be created in which
spiritual growth is possible, providing solitary quiet
and serenity in the midst of busy Western lives. It
must be a retreat conducive to profound thought,
self-analysis, and the practice of spiritual discipline.
In such a setting the example of Christ can be
adapted to the Christian's life. Reading the Bible
and great Christian devotional classics or cultivating some form of the Christian artistic tradition
may serve as an avenue to the divine. In this way
Christians derive enormous inner strength for the
active part of their commitment.

Christians will find themselves active at the point
where their services are needed in the world. Each
Christian's sphere of service is different, just as
each Christian possesses unique talents. But all find
their place in giving a stated part of every week to
direct Christian work.

Christians do not need a new law to take the place
of the one from which Christ has set them free. Let
all Christians select the means of discipline best
suited to their own unique gifts and temperaments.
But the religious life is powerless without discipline.

8. Prayer becomes meditative and contemplative

Many attitudes of prayer have found a place in
the Christian tradition, but the most common practice is petition. Humanity asks and God grants.
However, regarding prayer largely as petition makes
God a kindly grandfather in the sky who dispenses
favors like some cosmic Santa Claus. In addition,
this kind of exchange with God is largely verbal.
Many Christians hunger for an experience of God
that is more direct than this largely verbal exchange. They want their prayer to be direct communion with God.

Meditative and contemplative prayer fosters the experience of oneness with God. Petition can leave the being of the person praying relatively untouched; meditation and contemplation cannot. However little it may be known by contemporary Christians, there is a long and great tradition of Christian meditative and contemplative practice. It deserves to be better known and to be made more available for Christians' use. There are manuals of contemplation and rich spiritual insights to be found in the works of Thomas a Kempis, Jakob Bohme, William Blake, Dionysius the Areopagite, Meister Eckhart, Jan Van Ruysbroeck, St. Bernard, St. John of the Cross, St. Teresa, and the Theologia Germanica, to name some of the best known.

Techniques of meditation have no special mystery about them.

1. Turn the mind and spirit away from all that distracts them. Christians may use yoga and Eastern meditative techniques or any other techniques that focus the mind on spiritual matters.

2. An attentive mind may then be turned to the study of scripture, the literature of contemplation, Christian poetry and hymnody, Christian art.

3. The spirit may further prepare itself by cultivating a sense of reverence, awe, and devotion. This attitude, which does not come easily to Westerners, is essential, because it is the womb in which expectancy is cradled. Expectancy is prayer as silence before God. Silent, reverent expectancy is the key to the discovery of God's presence in the world of nature and of humanity. God will disclose himself to those who still the noisiness of their busy lives and who wait and listen reverently for his coming.

4. The Christian may then approach God and meditate upon God's nature. The majesty and grandeur

of God can be worshiped in all the beauty and variety of creation, in divine attributes, and in God's persons as creator, redeemer, and sanctifier.

The practice of meditation and contemplation will vary widely among Christians because individual aptitudes vary widely. There is no one prescribed set of methods to use. For some body/mind techniques like yoga are effective; for others the Christian contemplative tradition; for others the indirect methods of Zen; for others reading the Bible; for others the discipline of logic and hard intellectual thinking about the faith; for still others the contemplation of great Christian art and music. There are degrees of understanding and attainment, and Christians should use what is most natural to their temperament. They may eventually learn to use all of these techniques, at different times, because each possesses some part of the truth. Instruction in all of them should be available in congregations.

The great popularity of meditative and contemplative techniques today leads Christians back to rediscover a great tradition of contemplative prayer in their own religious history. Perhaps, in turn, this will lead to a revitalization of Christian practice of the presence of God in the 20th century.

9. Cultivating the bodily dimension of life

In the resurgence of religion we see far greater concern for the bodily dimension of humanity than has been commonplace in Western religion. However, it would be difficult to find a clearer description of humanity's psychophysical unity than that found in biblical accounts of creation: "Then the Lord God formed man of dust from the ground, and breathed into his nostrils the breath of life; and man became a living being" (Gen. 2:7). Humanity's creation from the dust is the symbol for its continuity with the world of nature out of which it has come. Like the whole great family of animal life, humanity has a finite nature tied to earthly time and space, determined by its instincts and its environment, a product of the natural process. Breathed into that finite body is the infinite spirit of life. God's breath is the gift of spirit and humanity is a psychophysical whole. A human being is a confluence of body and spirit, a unity, an integrated whole.

In the ancient and medieval worlds the myth arose that humanity's spiritual nature was somehow "higher" than the bodily side of its life. As the seat of intelligence and morals, the spiritual nature became the particular province of religion, while the bodily dimension of life was left to others.

The difficulty with such a view is that it ignores the psychophysical unity of humanity. It ignores the fact that the body is the means through which humanity communicates with the world, by which it is connected with it, adapted to it, and conditioned by it. The body is the basis of all experience, including that of the spirit, and the whole history of an individual's psychic reality is recorded in the body.

Ignoring the bodily side of human experience leads to failure in understanding men and women and their needs. Much of what happens in the spiritual or religious life of an individual is conditioned by physical factors. It can be argued, in fact, that modern humanity has ignored its physical side to its peril. The machine age, and particularly the advent of the automobile, has sometimes made it appear that humanity no longer needs the body. But the psychophysical consequences of abuse of the body and failure to use the body have been serious.

Christians can minister to people's bodies as well

as their spirits. Christians can take the lead in teaching athletic conditioning of the body, making provision for hard physical labor, yoga, control of diet and fasting, natural foods free of the synthetic substances of modern chemistry, a vegetarian diet for some, limiting the intake of alcohol and tobacco. In this way Christians would accept responsibility for providing strong and healthy spirits in strong and healthy bodies, and the "whole person" of Christians would benefit.

10. A guide to the realm of the spirit

The great success of Oriental gurus and roshis in the West today points to a need their leadership is meeting which perhaps Christians have not fully understood. A number of the themes we have been studying meet at this point: the common desire for primary experience and not verbal description of religious experience, the importance of a specific spiritual discipline, and the need for an experienced guide in spiritual matters.

People are saying they don't want to be told, they want to be shown. Christian leaders have not often been exemplary in the past. The Catholic view of leadership has accented the proper administration of the sacraments. The Protestant view of leadership has emphasized the interpretation of the Word of God in teaching and preaching. Neither has expected teaching by example.

At the same time, Christians have exceptionally strong resources for exercising effective leadership. The life of Jesus and the centrality of his experience of God for Christians is one such resource. However, for it to be effective, Jesus must be treated biographically rather than theologically. Christians will need to teach the humanity of Jesus as a model for people's humanity. They will need to bridge the gap between the rather remote, "stained glass" figure and his people. This is not at all to diminish his divinity, but rather to picture him in terms which Christians can find believable and understandable in their own experience.

The humanity of Jesus has often been virtually denied in the theological process of creating an all-powerful Lord in the heavens. The consequence is a great gulf between Christians as sinners and Jesus as divine. Christians have been taught so effectively that they are sinners that they would not even consider trying to be like Jesus. But a divine Son of God, remote in the heavens, cannot meet the current need for an exemplary leader.

In much the same way, the Christian priest or minister can exercise an exemplary leadership not envisioned in the past. Historically Christians have argued that their leaders' religious experience or lack of it did not validate their right to leadership, but instead ordination or knowledge of scripture. It may now be necessary to recognize more fully one of the fundamental truths of all leadership, that you cannot lead where you have not been yourself. You can only lead others into depths of spiritual experience you have plumbed. This may well require Christian pastoral leaders and their educators to place far greater emphasis on spiritual discipline and the experience of the inner world. Time will need to be provided busy pastors for the cultivation of their own spiritual gardens. How quickly one grows empty when there has been no opportunity for replenishing personal spiritual resources.

A new age may then require a new concept of Christian ministry, better equipped to guide and direct the inner spiritual voyage of Christian people.

11. Living harmoniously with nature

One of the great strengths of the resurgence of religion is that it is directing humanity back to its roots in nature after a long period of alienation caused by modern technological society. Since the dawn of the industrial revolution, society has viewed nature as its workshop. Nature was seen as resources intended to contribute to humanity's well-being, for people to manipulate and dispose of to serve their purposes.

Christians, who have baptized Western capitalism and industrialization too uncritically, can join the new religions in urging others to develop a life-style that is more harmonious with humanity's natural environment. Modern humanity must no longer feel antagonistic to the world, but instead one with it. Women and men belong to the natural world, from which they draw their sustenance and meaning, in harmony, unity, and wholeness. This kind of relationship is similar to that which animals have with their environment, a symbiotic relationship of natural dependency.

Ingredients in this harmony are nature's rhythms, which recur with unfailing regularity: the movements of sun and moon, planets and stars, night following day, the rotation of the seasons, the process of growth and decay. Nature's measured motions are seen in the orderly rising and setting of the sun, in the ebb and flow of a great river, in the coming of rain and sunshine for crops, in a bird in flight and at rest, in autumn becoming winter.

That harmony can be created in a Christian's personal life in such a way as to reflect nature's larger harmony. People can find happiness and enjoyment in experiencing the cycle of their years. For everything there is a season and a time: a time for youth and a time for age, a time for labor and a time for rest, a time for joy and a time for tears, a time for beauty in the eye and a time for eternity in the soul.

It is ironic that Christians should be pointed back to the first article of their creed (God the Father as creator) by the trends of current religion. There has been a tendency for them to concentrate on the second article (God the Son as redeemer), while charismatic Christians emphasize the third (God the Holy Spirit as sanctifier).

But the first article can only be neglected at the Christian's peril, because nature leads people to regard nature's maker. Nature's great beauty and its marvelous intricacy lead people to wonder and to ponder their creator. People find evidence of God in nature's ceaseless creativity in producing the unforeseen, and in its intelligibility, which makes the whole enterprise of modern science possible. This is not a world devoid of God, but rather one which displays many evidences of divine presence.

It is because people in industrial society are so remote from Eden that they no longer ask about Eden's maker. Everyone knows that humans have built the modern machine world. It is more difficult to ask the God question on the floor of a busy factory surrounded by all the symbols of human inventiveness. Returning to Eden and discovering the old harmony anew, however, raises persistent questions about Eden's maker.

> For what can be known about God is plain. . . .
> Ever since the creation of the world his invisible
> nature, namely, his eternal power and deity,
> has been clearly perceived in the things that
> have been made (Rom. 1:19-20).

Adherents of the resurgence of religion do not appear to ask the God question very clearly. But perhaps in leading people back to nature, the movement may lead them to rediscover the being of God anew. I believe many Christians will follow the same path and discover God in the things he has made.

A clear picture emerges then of how Christians may meet the present challenge of the invasion from the East. They can:

1. Proclaim their faith in the one God who stands at the center and thereby give a center to others, and emphasize a more mystical conception of God without losing God's personal characteristics.

2. Rediscover the rich tradition of Christian mysticism and its practice, and teach it to other mystics as a further stage to be reached.

3. Listen anew to Jesus' disregard for material well-being as a goal for life and help liberate people from the entanglements of materialistic society.

4. Recognize that there are diverse paths of salvation, and so meet a broader spectrum of people's needs.

5. Frame a more optimistic doctrine of humanity, and teach Christian self-transcendence to those Westerners attracted by the religions of the East.

6. Place a greater emphasis on the dimension of personal experience and recover spontaneity.

7. Make a larger place in their lives for the practice of a daily spiritual discipline and the discipleship of Christ.

8. Rediscover and practice their own tradition of contemplative and meditative prayer.

9. Minister to the "whole person" of their people and take the lead in schooling them in holding the faith in strong and healthy bodies.

10. Develop a new leadership better able to guide people on the inner spiritual voyage.

11. Enrich their doctrine of the creation and teach their people a greater appreciation for and relationship with the world of nature.

Notes

Chapter 1

1. Martin Heidegger, *Existence and Being* (Chicago: Henry Regnery Co., 1949), p. 289.
2. Melvin Maddocks, "America's Therapy Industry," *Christian Science Monitor*, 10 January 1977, pp. 14-15; and Kenneth Woodward, "Getting Your Head Together," *Newsweek*, 6 September 1976, pp. 56-62.
3. David Miller, *The New Polytheism* (New York: Harper and Row, 1974), chap. 1.
4. For two descriptive surveys of these groups see Robert Ellwood Jr., *Religious and Spiritual Groups in Modern America* (Englewood Cliffs, N.J.: Prentice-Hall, 1973); and Jacob Needleman, *The New Religions* (New York: Pocket Books, 1972).
5. Maddocks, "America's Therapy Industry," pp. 14-15.
6. Robert Bellah, "New Religious Consciousness and the Crisis in Modernity," in *The New Religious Consciousness*, Charles Glock and Robert Bellah, eds. (Berkeley, Calif.: University of California Press, 1976), p. 338.
7. Bellah, "New Religious Consciousness," p. 338.
8. Bellah, "New Religious Consciousness," p. 341.

Chapter 2

1. *The Upanishads*, Juan Mascaro, trans. (New York: Penguin, 1965), p. 101.
2. In *Upanishads*, Mascaro, trans., p. 114.
3. William James, *The Varieties of Religious Experience* (New York: Random, 1902), p. 371.

4. *The Word of the Buddha,* compiled and translated by Thera Nyanatiloka, Colombo, Sri Lanka, English translation by J. F. M'Kechnie, 1907, quoted in Christmas Humphreys, *The Wisdom of Buddhism* (New York: Harper and Row, 1960), p. 66.

5. Kenneth Keniston, "Drug Use and Student Values," in *Religion for a New Generation,* Jacob Needleman, et al. (New York: Macmillan, 1973), pp. 29-30.

6. *Anguttara-Nikaya,* Devamitta Thera, ed. (Colombo, Sri Lanka, 1929), quoted in Walpola Rahula, *What the Buddha Taught* (New York: Grove Press, 1959), pp. 2-3.

7. *Vimansaka-Sutta* of the *Majjhima-Nikaya* (Pali Text Society), cited in Rahula, *What the Buddha Taught,* p. 3.

8. Needleman, et al., *Religion for a New Generation,* p. 339.

9. Ellwood, *Religious and Spiritual Groups,* p. 17.

Chapter 3

1. *Bhagavad Gita* 10.20-41, A. L. Basham, trans., in *The Wonder That Was India* (New York: Grove Press, 1954), p. 301.

2. *Chandogya Upanishad* 6.12, in *Upanishads,* Mascaro, trans., p. 117.

3. *Svetasvatara Upanishad,* Swami Prabhavananda and F. Manchester, trans., in *The Upanishads: Breath of the Eternal* (New York: Mentor Books, 1957), pp. 123-25.

4. *Chandogya Upanishad* 6.14, in *Upanishads,* Mascaro, trans., p. 118.

5. *Svetasvatara Upanishad,* 3, in *Upanishads,* Mascaro, trans., pp. 89-90.

6. *Brihad-Aranyaka Upanishad* 3.7, Walter Kaufman, trans., in *Religions in Four Dimensions* (New York: Reader's Digest Press, 1976), p. 219.

7. *Bhagavad Gita* 2.47-48, Juan Mascaro, trans. (Baltimore: Penguin, 1962), p. 52.

8. *Bhagavad Gita* 18.45-46, R. C. Zaehner, trans. (London: Oxford University Press, 1969), p. 106.

9. *Bhagavad Gita,* Zaehner, trans., pp. 17-19.

10. *Bhagavad Gita* 3.3, 3.8, 3.19, 3.25, Zaehner, trans., pp. 54-55.

11. *Bhagavad Gita* 6.27, 6.29, Zaehner, trans., p. 67.

12. *Bhagavad Gita* 18.64-66, Zaehner, trans., p. 108.

13. *Bhagavad Gita* 6.34-35, Mascaro, trans., p. 72.

14. *Bhagavad Gita* 6.11-13, 5.27-28, 6.14-15, Zaehner, trans., p. 433.

15. *Bhagavad Gita* 2.58, Zaehner, trans., p. 52.
16. *Bhagavad Gita* 6.18-29, Zaehner, trans., pp. 66-67.

Chapter 4

1. *The First Sermon*, Vinaya Texts, in *Sacred Books of the East*, vol. 13, T. W. Rhys Davids and Herman Oldenberg, trans. (Oxford: Clarendon, 1883), p. 94; quoted in John Noss, *Man's Religions*, 5th ed. (New York: Macmillan, 1974), p. 125.
2. *Some Sayings of the Buddha*, F. L. Woodward, trans. (London: Oxford University Press, 1925), p. 30; quoted in Humphreys, *Wisdom of Buddhism*, p. 42.
3. *The Buddha's Philosophy*, G. F. Allen, trans. (Reading, Mass.: Allen and Unwin, 1958), pp. 154-56; quoted in Humphreys, *Wisdom of Buddhism*, pp. 93-94.
4. *Anguttara-Nikaya*, Devamitta Thera, ed. (Colombo, Sri Lanka, 1929), p. 115; quoted in Rahula, *What the Buddha Taught*, pp. 2-3.
5. "The Rock Edict," 12, in Rahula, *What the Buddha Taught*, pp. 4-5.
6. *Majjhima-Nikaya*, 1 (Pali Text Society), pp. 134-35, quoted in Rahula, *What the Buddha Taught*, pp. 10-11.

Chapter 5

1. Holmes Welch, *Taoism*, rev. ed. (Boston: Beacon Press, 1957), pp. 35ff.
2. Christmas Humphreys, *Buddhism* (London: Penguin, 1951), p. 182.
3. Humphreys, *Buddhism*, p. 180.
4. Alan Watts, *The Way of Zen* (New York: Random House, 1957), p. 134.
5. Daisetz Suzuki, *Zen and Japanese Culture* (New York: Princeton University Press, 1959), p. 353.
6. Suzuki, *Zen and Japanese Culture*, pp. 353-58.
7. Noss, *Man's Religions*, p. 169.
8. Alan Watts, *The Spirit of Zen* (New York: Grove Press, 1958), pp. 69-70.
9. Watts, *Spirit of Zen*, p. 79.
10. Humphreys, *Buddhism*, p. 185.
11. Daisetz Suzuki, *Essays in Zen Buddhism*, 3 (New York: Grove Press, 1961), pp. 88ff., cited in Heinrich Dumoulin, *A History of Zen Buddhism* (Boston: Beacon Press, 1963), p. 39.

12. Blake, William, *The Portable Blake* (New York: Viking, 1946), p. 150.
13. Suzuki, *Zen and Japanese Culture*, p. 356.
14. Daisetz Suzuki commenting on Basho, Zen's most famous poet, in Erich Fromm, Daisetz Suzuki, and Richard de Martino, *Zen Buddhism and Psychoanalysis* (New York: Harper and Row, 1960), p. 85.
15. Langdon Warner, "Gardens," in Nancy Wilson Ross, *The World of Zen* (New York: Vintage, 1960), p. 110.

Chapter 7

1. Augustine, *Confessions* I. 2-3, quoted in A. C. McGiffert, *A History of Christian Thought*, vol. 2 (New York: Scribner's, 1954), p. 84.
2. See Evelyn Underhill, *Practical Mysticism* (New York: E. P. Dutton, 1915), pp. 87-147; and R. C. Zaehner, *Mysticism Sacred and Profane* (New York: Oxford University Press, 1957), p. 168.
3. A. L. Basham, "Hinduism," in *The Concise Encyclopedia of Living Faiths*, R. C. Zaehner, ed. (Boston: Beacon Press, 1959), p. 230.
4. Bellah, *New Religious Consciousness*, pp. 340-41.
5. *Religion for a New Generation*, p. 12.
6. *The Church of the Savior* (2025 Massachusetts Ave. NW, Washington, D.C.: The Church of the Savior), p. 1.